GRATEFUL
PUBLISHING

Five Minutes With

GOD

A simple way to relax and reconnect with your Creator

Rev. Terri Linnea Meigs

www.revterri.org

Five Minutes With GOD
Copyright 2020 by Rev. Terri Linnea Meigs

ISBN: 978-17344990-6-3

~ DEDICATION ~

I dedicate this work to God
and to my loving parents
and supportive friends.
This is also dedicated to
you, the reader.
Thank you for being on this
spiritual journey with me.

CHAPTER ONE
WHY THIS BOOK
AND HOW TO USE IT

> *Be not afraid. We only start again an*
> *ancient journey long ago begun*
> *that but seems new. We have begun*
> *again upon a road we traveled on*
> *before*
> *and lost our way a little while. And*
> *now we try again.*
> *~ A Course In Miracles*

First thing first.

You are not reading a book.

No, this is my humble and heartfelt love letter to the world, and especially to YOU, my dear reader. For about nine months, all my spare energy went into writing this for you. I have felt your presence as I wrote each word. You didn't know it until now, but your energy helped me keep going even when it was difficult. The world is going through some trying times lately. We need a few moments of peace and serenity more than ever before. This sacred place is one of bridges instead of walls. Through our willingness to learn meditation we create unity instead of divisions.

In just five minutes a day, we can connect to our Creator, in whatever way we understand Him. In this way, we become connected, soul to soul, in a world that often separates people. No matter how far apart we may be, in physical space and time, I know you are encouraging me to write this book. So, it must be that I am there, with you also.

This isn't some new-age twaddle. This connection is real.

That's why I want to be crystal clear that this is for you, wherever you are. I promise it will be worth your while. Please know that I am not any kind of guru or saint. Not even close. I am just a simple person who has changed for the better because of forty years of daily meditation. I am still growing and changing, and I am not perfect. For example, please forgive me if I repeat myself, have little typos, make a few silly jokes or even, have the occasional grammatical errors. Forgive me also, for my opinions outnumber my citations by far.

For all my imperfections, I am well-intentioned. I would like to help you build a meditation practice that is easy and simple. If I use a phrase or term that puts you off or doesn't apply to your situation, please just press on. Hold off judgment until you have read the whole thing. Some concepts will be explained in greater depth later on. Please don't let any of that make you put the book down. Just keep reading. I have intentionally made this book short so that even if you hate it, it will all be over soon. That's supposed to get a laugh, by the way. You might as well know right away that I believe it is okay to be spiritual and laugh.

I promise that whether you are new to meditation, or you have been doing it for years, my simple technique will help you. Meditation will enhance your life in ways you can't even imagine right now. So, don't let a word or two throw you off the path. You are about to start a journey full of love and miracles.

Up until now, I have only shared this technique with close friends. For example, awhile back, my beautiful friend Annabelle (not her real name) told me she wanted to begin a meditation practice. She is active in an "Anonymous" program and for obvious reasons, I won't disclose any more than that. As many people know, the Twelve Steps consist of a rigorous and supportive plan of self-discovery. Annabelle had come a long way in her recovery and was just beginning to work on the "Eleventh Step." I obtained this important quote from the AA website[1].

 The Eleventh Step states: "Sought through prayer and meditation to improve our conscious contact with God as we understood Him, praying only for knowledge of His will for us and the power to carry that out." (2)

Wow! That is brilliant!

Whether we are in a program or not, this is something we can all aspire to. Furthermore, it is the premise of this entire book.

To continue, Annabelle already had a good daily prayer practice, which she used religiously. (Sorry, couldn't help it!) Now,

---

[1] (https://www.aa.org/pages/en)

she wanted to learn more about meditation. She wasn't sure where to begin. There are so many how to choose and then start a meditation practice. There are so many options, and so many different schools of thought, practices, and techniques. It can be a bit overwhelming. Annabelle remembered that I liked to meditate every day, so we had a good talk. In just a few minutes, I shared a meditation technique with her that has worked wonders for me, for many years. She had the whole thing down pat in just a few minutes. It really is that easy! About a month later, she told me that she adapted my technique slightly to meet her specific needs. This is perfectly fine. She said that overall, her new meditation practice was going very well.

The main thing is this - she was willing to try something new, in order to get a better result. I gave her just one more tool to help her. To be clear, I am not affiliated with, nor am I endorsed by any twelve-step program because that is the way their policy works. I simply strive to make this book an added resource to anyone who is working on their spiritual life.

I started to wonder if other people are looking for a deeper connection to God or their Higher Power. Helping people is my sole purpose in life. (If you don't like puns, I'm so sorry!) Anyway, this book is meant to be just one more tool in your spiritual toolbox. If it doesn't work for you, that's okay, too. I simply offer up this meditation technique, which was given to me by some Divine Inspiration. You have been inspired to pick it up. Now that we are connected in this way, we are ready to learn from each other.

I promise that if you give this meditation practice an honest try, you will gain something from it. The technique I am about to share is not attached to any religion or school of thought. If you are Jewish, Buddhist, Muslim, Pagan, or any other faith, this technique can easily be added into it, as you see fit. And, when I say "God" you can substitute the word that matches your faith tradition. If you are Agnostic or Atheist, this meditation technique will also help you. In that case, you can substitute the term Universal Energy when I say "God."

I will go into this more later, but my use of the word God and male pronouns is just to make communication easier. For me, the word God points to or alludes to "The Great Mystery" or "Creator of All Things." I believe God is bigger than either the male or female gender, in the way we understand this here on earth. Regardless of your race, religion, background, sexual orientation, or gender identification, meditation will help you. No matter your education or profession, or busy schedule this will help you. Even if you don't practice a religion, meditation will help you. This practice is an all-inclusive package. Everyone is welcome with open arms.

I also promise that anyone can do this meditation technique, regardless of your cognitive or physical abilities, or mobility issues. You do not need to sit on the floor, with your legs crossed. You do not need to choose between your spiritual development and the circulation in your legs. I used to sit in the lotus pose until my feet fell asleep. I can't do that anymore even if I wanted to! For this technique, you do not have to attain any certain pose. You don't need to perform certain rituals or chant special mantras given to you by a guru. Except for a few deep breaths to start with, you don't have to use specific breathing techniques. Normal breathing is fine. To be clear, there is nothing wrong with any of these things if they work for you. Yet, for our purposes, the only thing required is five minutes of dedicated and heartfelt effort.

There are very few "rules" here. One of them is this: you must be willing to do this every day for at least thirty days. If at the end of thirty days, this is not your cup of tea, then just give the book to someone else. I believe that in just a month, you will notice great rewards. I may sound like a salesman, but yes, in just five minutes a day, you will feel more relaxed and have a deeper spiritual connection. But wait, there's more! You may also experience lower stress which may improve physical conditions caused by stress. Yes, I sound like a salesman but rest assured, the only thing I am selling is inner peace.

I can almost hear you ask, "What do you mean, 'five minutes with God'? That sounds kinda nuts. Can anything really meaningful happen in just five minutes?"

The answer is "Yes!" And I can prove it. I would like to answer your question by inviting you to try a simple imagination exercise. Take a moment to think about your favorite famous person from the world of music, film, business, politics, or sports. Someone you have always wanted to meet. Your most beloved rock star or actress. The richest man in the world. Or the President of the United States. Choose anyone you want. Really hold the image of that person in your mind. Now, imagine you won some kind of "biggest fan" contest or something. This important and notable person has agreed to meet you. They will carve out a little bit of time and give their undivided attention to you. During these few minutes, you can ask questions and share everything that is in your heart. He or she will listen, with great love and attentiveness. He or she will calmly and lovingly explain things that you have always wanted to know. In a relaxed and personal way, this amazing person will be dedicated to you and only you for five minutes.

Think about it, who comes to mind? Who would you want to meet?

Perhaps you want to meet the quarterback from the winning Super Bowl team. Or an inspirational figure from the WNBA. Now, imagine that this person is standing on your doorstep, knocking at your door, asking you to make some time for him or her. After you are done gushing about how much you admire them, you can ask them anything. You might ask, "What is it like to train for so many years and then win so big? Do you have any special physical, mental, or emotional tactics that helped you become such a big winner?" It would be amazing to be with someone like that, even just for a few minutes. The information and inspiration you could acquire from this brief encounter could change your life forever. So, even if you were super busy, wouldn't you rearrange your schedule to meet with this person? Well, God is a bigger winner than any sports figure.

Okay, maybe you are not into sports, but you want to develop your wealth. Imagine someone like Warren Buffet is knocking on your door. He has agreed to spend five minutes with you, in private. He will answer all your questions about how and where to invest. Think about that! Just one visit from him could result in greater wealth for you and your family for years to come. Now imagine he wants to meet with you a little while each day. How much would it be worth to meet with him for even just five minutes, every day? Even if you had to slightly change your daily routine, you would be crazy to give up such an opportunity. Well, God is a million times richer and more successful than any businessman or woman! Now, I am not promising that if you meditate you will become rich. But it sure won't make you poor.

Some people would rather meet their favorite actor or musician. I know it sounds outlandish, but what if your most beloved star is knocking on your door. He or she heard about you somehow and wants to meet *you*! Robert De Niro, or Meryl Streep, or Bono or your favorite Hip Hop star is right there on your doorstep. He or she is hoping you will let them in for a few minutes. Would you stand on the other side of your door and ignore them? I highly doubt you would say, "Sorry, but I'm super busy right now. Come back another time!" No, I don't think so. If such a talented and creative person sat with you, even for just five minutes a day, it would probably enhance your life tremendously. You already know what I'm gonna say. God is more talented and creative than any person on this planet.

Awhile back, I watched a documentary called The Bill Murray Experience (2017) which was written and directed by actress Sadie Katz. (3) This super fan desperately wanted to meet Bill. She spent an entire year of her life doing anything to get just five minutes of his time! She dressed up in crazy unicorn costumes and bought dozens of balloons to give him. She spent hours planning trips to odd places where he might be, from golf events to private parties. She stopped everything – her whole life - to attend all these random events. (I don't know why she thought Bill would respond to any of this!) I think Bill Murray is cool, but he's just a human being, flaws, and all. Yet, here is the point. What if she had spent that year and all that money and effort toward a greater relationship with her Creator? What if each one of us were that dedicated to finding God and spending a just few minutes with Him? Our connection to God would become even deeper, surely. Yes, I am sure that five minutes with Bill Murray would be lots of fun. You might end up with a cute picture with him if you are lucky. But five minutes a day with God will give you the "peace that passeth all understanding." How much would *that* be worth to you?

I have been very blessed to meet several famous people. I don't *try* to make it happen, which is the key to how it happens. My mom was in politics so even at a young age, I met a few powerful senators and governors from Connecticut. As I got older and developed a deep love for music, literature, and spirituality, I met Ram Dass, Gregg Allman, Robert Hunter, Alan Ginsberg, Ray Manzarek, and Ken Kesey, to name just a few. These moments were brief, but they have remained with me and are of huge significance, for all my life. From experience, I can assure you, that "meeting" God in meditation is way better!

Even now, I would love to meet a lot of cool people from every walk of life. This list changes all the time. Right now, some of my favorites would be Jamie Foxx, Andrew Cuomo, Meryl Streep, Eddie Vedder, and Oprah Winfrey. Weird combination, to be sure. It would be so amazing to spend just five minutes with any of them. I would ask some deep questions and hopefully, also enjoy a few hugs and laughs. Such an experience would live in my heart forever. Well, I think by now you get the point: the same is true of just five minutes with God. And, the great thing is, God (however you define Him) wants to be with you, too.

So, take a moment. If you would love to spend five minutes with an actress, rich guy, or sports figure, then think about spending five minutes a day with God. Isn't God (or Great Mystery, or whatever term you prefer) isn't God more important and interesting? If you don't agree, then you should put the book down right now and give it away, because you are not ready for this. For those of us who are still reading, let's explore this concept a little.

By now you agree that your Creator has more wisdom, creativity, humor, and greater prosperity than any human being, ever. If you follow this super-easy meditation program, I guarantee that you will develop a deeper relationship with this Entity or Force, however you perceive it.

Also, I believe that you, yes, YOU are every bit as important as any rich or famous person. Consider the time you spend in meditation to be a time to know yourself better. Aren't you worth it? Yes. Yes, you are! I promise that if you devote just five minutes, every day, you will reap unbelievable rewards. You will not only reduce stress, but you will gain insights and reconnect with your Creator.

HOW TO USE THIS BOOK

I would like to offer an important suggestion. You can easily read this little book from cover to cover in a few hours. Go ahead and do that if you like. If you do, I recommend you read it again in a slower, in a more measured, and meditative way. I recommend reading the book one chapter at a time. Then do the exercises at the end, then document or jot down notes from any impressions you may have felt. Read one chapter a day this way. Let me explain.

First, choose a time when you would like to meditate. Some people prefer first thing in the morning before everyone else is awake. Or, at night when it is nice and quiet. Any time you have some uninterrupted time will be fine. Try to keep to the same time each day. If you try mornings and that doesn't work, it's no problem. Just pick another time and try that. Do this until you know what feels right for you. Then stick to that time period from now on as you read the book.

Similarly, find a comfortable, cozy place to sit. This is the first step to the technique I will share with you soon. It is called "Get Comfy." Not too difficult, right? All you have to do is make sure you feel supported in your chair without having to think about it. If you can do this with a straight spine, that is ideal. I don't recommend lying down on a bed or being in the same spot where you sleep. Yet, get comfortable. You don't get any points in Heaven for feeling awkward.

Then, I suggest you read just one chapter a day, trying not to skip a day, if you can help it. This will take you nine days. After you're done with each chapter, relax and reflect on it a few minutes.

Re-read the inspirational quotes that come at the beginning and end of each chapter. Imagine some of the greatest teachers the world - whispering directly in your ear. Think about how these quotes apply to your life. What do you find most meaningful? Jot down any thoughts or feelings that come up.

Lastly, work on the exercises that have been specially designed for each chapter. You can do them in your head, but I recommend that you write down your thoughts, impressions, and feelings in the margins. The exercises are designed to give you some time to process what you have read. This brief period of reflection will be similar to the meditation practice itself.

I will say that the exercises are easy, but they can be thought-provoking. Write down your feelings and impressions. Have fun with it. Doodle in the margins. If something comes up that you don't like it's even more important to write that down. Please don't try to keep the book spotless or "nice." Make it messy. This book is your journal – it is documentation of your spiritual development. In this way, you become a co-author with me.

At some point after each exercise, close your eyes and simply relax. Let your mind wander. Be open to whatever comes up for you. Don't try to make anything happen or to avoid anything from happening.

Side story, in the early 1990's I followed the great spiritual teacher Ram Dass around for a few lectures in California. He spoke a great deal of being of service, especially to those who were sick or dying. As always, he spent a lot of time after each lecture hugging anyone who waited patiently in line for it. I had gone to a couple of these lectures and when it came my turn for a hug, he recognized me. He looked at me with piercing blue eyes that saw directly into my soul. He had a little smile, as if he saw something in me that either amused him or pleased him. He asked me to tell him a little bit about why I was there, why I was there *again*, what I needed from his lectures. I told him I had loved him ever since reading Be Here Now (4) as a teenager. He nodded as if to say, "And? And?" So, I opened up and said I was starting a new career as a preschool teacher. I was having a hard time with a little girl who wouldn't take a nap. He listened intently and I felt he understood the situation completely. Then he got close to my face and said, "Just be the Divine Witness for her, whatever she is going through. You were not put on this planet to "fix" her, but to *be there* for her. Be that peaceful presence she has been waiting for. Show her the *quality* of calmness instead of trying to *"make"* her calm. Be the Divine Witness for her." That was the best advice I ever received as a teacher, a caregiver and as a person. Now, I take the precious gift of his advice and I offer it to you.

Be the Divine Witness for yourself and your own spiritual development. Allow yourself to take a break from being the almighty judge and jury of what you think and feel. For just five minutes, give yourself permission to let it all flow, without self-criticism. During this time, you are creating certain energy that will be used for the meditation practice we will do later on. This energy can best be described as relaxed but "elevated." Cultivate a feeling of being awake and aware and yet completely relaxed. Allow yourself to enjoy a few minutes of higher consciousness. Bring your thoughts higher, toward a lofty place of eternal ideals, such as Truth, Unconditional Love, and Devotion. As you read each chapter and do the exercises afterward, just know that you are being lifted to a place that is above your normal daily routine. Make it special. Then open your eyes and jot down whatever came up, even if it's just a word or two.

Read a chapter a day like this, until the book is finished. This daily pattern will help you develop a consistent habit that is needed for your new meditation practice. You will feel more relaxed, but at the same time, more spiritually energized. Take that energy out into the world and let it help you in your daily life. Or, if you prefer meditating at night, it may help you to relax fully and sleep better. The time and place you choose are based on whatever feels right.

I know that starting anything new is not always easy or comfortable at first. The best way to start a new adventure is to begin. New meditation practice is like starting a new work-out routine. Your ability to focus and meditate is like a muscle.

Ajahn Brahm said, "Meditation is like a gym in which you develop the powerful mental muscles of calm and insight." (5) Reading this book in this daily, measured way will get you into the "gym" of the mind and spirit.

If you work out a little every day, the time will come when you need to run to catch a bus or a toddler or lift something into your car, and you will be able to do so easily. Similarly, reading and reflecting a few minutes each day will make your "meditation muscles" grow and develop naturally. Each day, you will become more and more in alignment with your True Self.

This brings me to an important point about the True Self or Higher Self. Each one of us has a True Self that is deep within us, all the time. No one, no matter how evil they may appear, is without a Higher Self. No one. Some people might call the True Self their soul or even use the term Holy Spirit. These terms are pointing to the same thing: our inner knowing, our inner wisdom. The True Self is always there, whether we listen to it or not. It always knows what is right and wrong. It can immediately sense those things, people, situations that are in connection with a Higher Power or Eternal Entity. And it can immediately sense those things, people, and situations that are *not* in connection with a Higher Power.

I am not a psychologist, but I think we can all agree that each person has a complex system of self-preservation and protection methods. We have unique personality traits, and private, sometimes painful personal histories. For simplicity sake, I will call all this stuff the "ego."

I don't believe that the ego is necessarily bad. I think of it as a complex knot of mechanisms or interconnected wheel-gears. The ego was designed to protect us from predators, and move us forward, building things, attaining things and get us ahead in the world. A healthy ego can help us succeed in whatever arena is most desired by our personality. This ego-driven energy helps us very much in the "workaday world" of our careers, gaining a mate, and even protecting our families. For some people that is business and for others it may be the formation of good on-going relationships. The area where each person wants to grow, develop, and succeed is not a problem. In fact, there is nothing intrinsically wrong with the ego-self at all.

An ego is just a tool in life, no better or worse than a screwdriver. In my meditation method the ego does not have to be eradicated or eliminated to be an enlightened spiritual person. This energy is not "bad" or evil unless it gets out of control and subjugates the Higher Self. Everyone, from the most wonderful saint to the worst business tycoon must become aware of this fine line.

You will know the ego has gotten out of control when important, eternal things such as

Love and Truth become secondary to personal ambitions. For example, the politician who cries "Fake News!" only when it is unflattering to him is not stupid. He knows the Truth with a capital "T." Or the millionaire who destroys a whole town with pollution from his mining company. He knows this causes cancer and disabilities in the townsfolk. Yet, he does it anyway, to gain more wealth for himself and his shareholders. This is the opposite of Love, with a capital L. These are extreme examples of how the ego-self can overpower the True Self. But every person has a True Self. It's always there, they just don't want listen to it. They don't want the True Self to be more important than their ego. They prefer to nurture their selfish needs over their spiritual needs.

There is an old Native American story about the "Two Wolves" which I have heard from more than one tribe. I will reference the

Cherokee version here. A young boy goes to his grandfather with a dilemma. He feels there are two wolves inside him, fighting for dominance within him.

One is cuddly and kind and the other is vicious. He asks what he should do about this. The grandfather says that "the one you feed" is the one who will thrive. (6)_Only you can decide if you will feed your True Self, with the nutrients of meditation. Or, will you feed your ego-self first?

Granted, most of us are not money-grubbing business tycoons. We are good people who try to feed the nice wolf who lives inside us. Almost all of us want to enjoy loving relationships and live in a healthy, happy community. And it wouldn't be horrible to enjoy a few fun vacations and have comfortable homes and a few nice things along the way. There is nothing wrong with any of that. Yet we also want to be part of something larger than our ego personalities.

We want something spiritual or meaningful, but we can't sit around in a burlap bag meditating in a cave all day. On some level, as inhabitants of this earthly plane, we need the ego-self. It helps us get up off the couch, put some clothes on, and go to work. Unfortunately, most of us have become obsessed with the whole task of getting up and going to work (whether paid or unpaid.) We get on a hamster wheel of getting up, working, eating, sleeping, and going to work again. Many of us start to believe that is all there is. It is not. The "rat race" is just one aspect of life. The True Self knows that earthly success will come and go. It will rise and fall. If you picked up this book, then you know there is something higher – something eternal in life. Meditation is the key to keeping everything in balance.

Let me explain this with another imagination exercise. Imagine, if you will, that your entire life is like a song. For most of your day to day activities, you hum along with your particular song. Your tune remains more or less in a mid-range of notes, say around the middle C. There will be high notes and low notes in the melody. This makes the song, and your life interesting. Well, this is all fine and good. This little tune helps get you through school, do well at your job, and helps you endure through tough times. Yet, every now and then you hear a higher sound. It is as if a flute is being played off in the distance. It seems to be an octave above your daily song. Sometimes this higher sound is quiet and barely noticeable. Yet sometimes, during certain points in your life, this resounds like the thundering climax of Ode to Joy. It is strong enough to remind you of your True Self. In these moments of sublime understanding, you are lifted above your daily existence. This is the sound of your Higher Self. It is an octave above the personality, mind, ego, or "workaday" self. This beautiful, uplifting song reconnects you to something real and unwavering. It reminds you of your eternal Divinity.

Well, meditation, even for just five minutes a day, keeps that song going. It helps you to tune into these subtle sensations and intuitions. It helps you keep a good connection between your Higher Self and your ego.

Let's talk about a specific example. Your Higher Self knows it is vitally important to get enough sleep. You know that when you do, you feel so much better. Yet, late at night, almost every night, you decide to watch one more TV show or have one more little snack. So, you don't get to bed until midnight, again. You wake up feeling horrible and wonder why you did that. While your True Self understands the importance of sleep, your ego-mind can be like a willful toddler who doesn't want to go to bed.

In the same way, the True Self knows that meditation has many health and spiritual benefits. Yet, your mind will come up with all kinds of excuses not to do it. "I don't have time, or a quiet place or meditation is just too boring, or I've tried it and don't like it." These excuses are a normal sign of the ego-mind at work. Your ego-mind is telling you one thing and the True Self is telling you something else.

To deal with this, you can try to be a harsh taskmaster and force your mind to obey. This may work for some people, but I, for one, rebel against this sort of thing. I believe the best way to get your mind in alignment with your True Self is to distract it. Like a crying baby, who calms down when you shake your keys in front of it, your mind is distracted by shiny things. This is my funny way of saying that if you put your mind to the task of reading one chapter at a time, you will trick your mind into developing a meditation practice.

To that end, as you read a little bit every day your mind will become more in alignment with your Higher Self. All you have to do is create a daily routine or pattern that feels comforting and relaxing for you. When you sit down to read, tell yourself, "This is my special time to turn off the rat race for a little while. This is my chance to learn something new, relax, and reconnect with my Creator." If you make this daily experience something you look forward to, like a glass of wine after dinner, then you will be more successful. And I can assure you, meditation is more relaxing than a glass of wine!

You will be amazed at how fast your mind will become accustomed to this habit. Before

you know it, you will be saying, "Shhhh…
don't tell my brain but we are already
meditating!"

Meditation is relaxing and even sometimes
fun. I do need to give a word of caution too.
It is also a very personal process of self-
exploration. For some people, this may bring
up difficult memories. This means your True
Self is ready for a healing experience. You
will always be in a peaceful setting while
meditating. So, consider this an opportunity
to offer love and healing to wounded parts of
your psyche, if they show up. Meditation can
be like a big hug for the mind. However, if
feelings become overwhelming, please seek
out appropriate mental health care. There are
no heroes in this process. Going it alone or
suffering in silence will not get you any closer
to Enlightenment. In fact, "toughing it out" is
a sure way to separate yourself from the peace
and serenity you most need. This book is not
meant to be a substitute for mental health

treatment. My only goal for you is to become as healthy and happy as you can be. If this is your intention too, please reach out for support if you need it.

This little book is simply my way of sharing my love and support with you. If you are reading this, you are ready to become the person you have always wanted to be. I applaud you for trying something new. We are connected here at this moment. Somewhere off in the distance I can hear a choir singing Ode to Joy.

"Your goal is not to battle with the mind, but to witness the mind."
Swami Muktananda

EXERCISE:

Our first exercise will be super easy. And, hopefully, fun and relaxing, too!

1) As I mentioned earlier, get in a comfortable position where you don't have to think about it or work to maintain it.
2) Just relax and in general, think about the main points you remember from this chapter.
3) In general, think about a few of the good things in your life that you are grateful for. Don't make a list or anything, but just *feel* the gratitude, for really anything at all that you appreciate in your life.
4) Now, close your eyes for at least 5 minutes. You can set your alarm if you want to, but if possible, just leave this time open-ended.
5) Let your mind wander, with no agenda and no obligation for anything. It's good to take a couple of deep breaths

at first, but otherwise, don't try to breathe in any certain way. Normal breathing is good. Don't try to make anything in particular happen. Allow yourself to simply BE. Simply witness yourself enjoying this time of peace and tranquility. There is no pressure to DO anything. When you are done with five minutes (or more if you had time) give thanks for this moment of connection to your Higher Power or however you imagine your Creator. That's it for now.

6) If anything came up for you, or you "saw" anything or heard anything, write it down. For example, some people see bright colors or hear a tone or sound of some kind. Some people have an emotion, or a random word will pop into their heads. Sometimes a warm or tingling sensation can occur, anywhere in the body. Other people suddenly have a friend or family member come up, for no

apparent reason. If any of these things happened, write it down immediately. However trivial it may seem, it is important. I will go more into this later.

7) Please know that the majority of people will just "see" a flat, dark color when they close their eyes. That is perfectly normal. Some might see a spot or streak of color. It is all good. You have done it perfectly.

8) Go about the rest of your day knowing that you just did a wonderful thing. You found a bit of relaxation today. You made steps toward a deeper connection with your True Self. Be at peace because everything is unfolding exactly as it should be.

CHAPTER TWO:
WHO IS GOD?
And why do we want to connect with Him? (And is God a "Him"?)

> *"When his life was ruined, his family killed, his farm destroyed, Job knelt down on the ground and yelled up to the heavens, "Why god? Why me?" and the thundering voice of God answered, there's just something about you that pisses me off."*
> ~ Stephen King, Storm of the Century

This quote brings up an important point. Although I take the subject matter very seriously, I believe meditation also brings a lot of joy and yes, sometimes even giggles. Your meditation practice does not have to be somber or dreary. Please do not take this as irreverence toward God. We can all just lighten up. That is what we are doing here on this planet: we are all becoming more enlightened.

Before we take another step on this journey, I feel the need to explain something vitally important to this entire book. I will go into more detail later, but I am an ordained Inter-Faith Minister. Since I was thirteen, I have studied and developed a great respect for the religions and spiritual practices of the world. I am still learning. I have come to feel that God is not an old white man who yells at us from the heavens. I use the word God only as a place marker to stand for something or an Entity or Force, which is ultimately indescribable. God is the Great Mystery of

Life. The ultimate Creator of all things. If someone says they can describe this dynamic force or entity with one perfect word, they are either much smarter than me or deluding themselves. I was brought up in a Christian family, so I am comfortable with the term "God" and using male pronouns.

I want to reiterate that I deeply respect all faiths. If you use words such as Allah, Adonai, Rama, or one of the hundred other names for "God" this meditation technique will still help you. Or, if you believe in a Divine Feminine, simply substitute feminine pronouns. Even if you aren't religious, this book will help you. Perhaps you practice a faith that does not specifically use a name for "God." I respect that, also. This is why I often use the term Creator. I think we can all agree some great energy created us. Some may call this Universal Energy. While I use God, and "Him" please simply substitute the terms and pronouns you feel comfortable using. The swap-out will not affect the value of the meditation practice I will teach you.

I believe God is bigger than all the words in the world, combined. There's no need to get hung up on little words when there is a big Word, that points to the Divine.

 Second Timothy 3:16 says, "In the beginning was the Word, and the Word was with God, and the Word was God." (2) That is a big concept to unpack! I ponder this one a lot. I believe that our Creator, the Force that created the entire universe is not petty or small. God would not want us to pause our spiritual development to quibble over a word or pronoun. Our human words come from our limited and human perspective which can never truly reflect the enormity of the Universe. God is neither male nor female in the human sense. God is Love. I believe our main job in life is to open up and learn how to accept all of this love. So, we must find some mutually agreeable way of discussing all this.

Therefore, use whatever terms and pronouns are respectful of your beliefs and traditions.

Perhaps you are a logical, scientific person. You are welcome here! Even the smartest scientists in the world agree there is always more to learn. No one has all the answers yet. There's still a lot of wonder and mystery at work in the universe.

As Shakespeare said, "There are more things in heaven and earth, Horatio, than are dreamt of in your philosophy." (3)

None of us know everything. Most agree that some energy or force created the universe. And it is still at work. This energy continues to flow through you, me, and all the plants and every animal on Earth. It flows through the millions of suns and planets that swirl in perfect orbit around those suns. In some mysterious way, this life-force connects everything and everyone, all the time. If you are a person who does not believe in God, perhaps you can believe in this awesome energy. Meditation will help you tap into all that amazing Universal Energy. It will tune your vibration to better match this Mysterious Force. If you don't believe in God, you will still get a lot from meditation.

All that matters is your willingness to jump into that Great Mystery. The Creator of the sun, moon, stars, and everything on Earth, including each one of us, is so happy that you are willing to learn something new. Your desire to be a more peaceful, loving person is the most wonderful thing. Meditation will help you gain greater clarity, relaxation, and peace of mind, no matter your religion or lack thereof.

I also use the Stephen King quote to offer a mirror so you can look at your vision of who God is or is not. Do you see God as an angry old man in "heaven" somewhere? Is God someone who will make you suffer if you don't live up to His lofty standards? Many people were brought up this way and still have vestiges of this way of thinking. If you still have any belief in a punishing God who arbitrarily favors one person over another, then your meditation practice will be sporadic and unsuccessful. The interesting thing is, even if you are *rebelling* against this idea, fighting against it, your meditation practice will also be sporadic and unsuccessful. This is because you are still putting energy into something that does not work for you. You can't split your energy and expect a unified result.

When we develop a meditation practice, we have to decide if we even want to connect with God, or Universal Energy. Some people have suffered what we can call a "spiritual injury." This means that something happened during their spiritual upbringing which causes pain. For some of us, the spiritual injury was getting our knuckles rapped on by a ruler-wielding nun. Or we were scolded by a minister for being naughty. Or we were scared by harsh, dogmatic sermons full of fire and brimstone. When someone begins to explore their sexuality, he or she might feel outcast from their Church, Mosque, Synagogue, or Temple. Furthermore, people who were sexually abused by clergy have a spiritual injury that can take years to heal.

If you grew up feeling that God doesn't love you for who you are, you would probably, and rather reasonably prefer to ignore God. You may tell yourself religion no longer matters. I have the utmost empathy for these deeply personal experiences. They are real and really important. I sincerely hope that anyone who has suffered will reach out to trusted resources. Let's just say that until you have found healing, you probably won't feel like getting closer to God, or a Higher Power. All you can do is to work on finding the Truth and giving yourself the love you need to heal. We all do, eventually.

Even if you personally have not had a spiritual leader abuse you, you may be aware of various spiritual injustices. In either case, many people are sensitive to various historical injustices. For example, the United States was influenced early on by the Puritans. They had wonderful qualities such as perseverance and adventure and devotion to God. Surviving in this new place was nothing short of a miracle, for which we can all be proud.

However, we have been taught a fairy tale version that the Native Americans and Puritans had a nice Thanksgiving, end of story. Their extreme religious views made many of new Americans believe that God gave them the right to kill witches and "savages," that is, Native American people. As they settled this great land they forgot one thing - the Native Americans were here first! As this country developed some people who called themselves Christians believed it was okay to use people - yes, *real people* - as free labor. How they arrived at this horrible conclusion is beyond me! The United States still suffers every day from the consequences of these tragedies. We need our schools to start teaching reality.

Whether we know it consciously or not, this is a spiritual injury that we have all endured, in one way or another. You may wonder why a Divine Being could allow for terrible things. There is an old saying that God didn't cause these things to happen – people did. Although none of us alive today were the ones who burned "witches" for example, we all must come to grips with this history, through brave acts of self-awareness and ultimately forgiveness.

I am not trying to put this country down, but I am trying to build our people back up. I love the United States of America. I am proud that my Ancestors fought in the Revolutionary and Civil Wars. My grandfather was awarded great honors, and suffered great injuries, from being a hero in World War I. I love this country so much that I want to heal the old spiritual injuries we deal with, in order to create a more perfect Union. The USA is a great place to live. We don't need to wear a red baseball cap to make this country is great again. It already is great.

Yet, let's not stop with the United States. Time and time again, one group of people believed their God told them to kill and displace other good people who had their own way of living and worshipping God. It is people - confused and greedy people - who used the concept of God as a weapon.

And now you have my book in your hands, and I am asking you to reconnect with God. A lot of people will feel a twinge of fear at this point. Who wants to "reconnect" with that kind of God? If we feel hesitation we will find numerous and clever ways to avoid God and also meditation. We will always be "too busy" or whatever. Excuses happen when you don't want to do something. If any part of us thinks God is going to punish us or banish us, then of course we will have mixed feelings. Everyone, on either side of a so-called victory, have a spiritual injury to deal with. The need for forgiveness is practically in our DNA. If you are sensitive to these things, eventually you will want to address the feelings you have about what has been done in God's name. It can take years to peel back that raw onion and shed some tears over these injustices. When you are ready, God is always ready to give and receive your forgiveness. Meditation can help.

I am here to tell you that no matter what happened, in the long run, you will be okay. You will survive and thrive. I am currently working on a book on Spiritual Injury and Forgiveness with a good friend of mine. We will explore this topic and offer some specific ideas and solutions. All I know for sure is that the only thing lacking in this world is self-awareness and true forgiveness. We need to acknowledge that an injury occurred and just to be clear, this is not a "blame game." It is simple honesty. Then we can forgive ourselves, other people, and God. And as you may have heard, we don't forgive for the other person's sake; we forgive them for our sake. Forgiveness is not condoning or allowing bad behavior. We are acknowledging and setting healthy boundaries. Then we can let go, and heal ourselves and others. The topic of forgiveness will also come up again later on because it applies in so many situations.

> *"What really matters, it seems to me, is a sincerity of intent to keep growing and deepening our spiritual work, and a strong commitment to keep walking our own unique path, will all of its challenges and wonders."*
> *~ Rev. Diane Berke,*
> *One Spirit Learning Alliance*

EXERCISE:

1. How do you describe God? Are you comfortable using male pronouns for your Creator? Why or why not.

2. Were you raised to believe in God? If not, describe your moral and ethical upbringing.

3. Have you experienced any kind of "spiritual injury"? If so, describe.

4. Are there many Gods and Goddesses in your spiritual practice? Do you have specific Deities based on your family tradition? In the margins here, describe the deity that you believe in.

5. If you don't have a belief in a specific deity, describe your Higher Power, feelings, or spiritual practice.

6. Do you believe in a Creative Force or
    Energy, rather than a personified
    deity? Try to describe your beliefs a
    little bit here.

CHAPTER THREE:
WHO ARE YOU?
WHO AM I?

When you meet anyone, remember it is a holy encounter.
As you see him you will see yourself.
As you treat him you will treat yourself.
~ A Course in Miracles

Now that we have given some thought to God or Life Force, let's concentrate on who you are for a moment. If you have picked up this book, from among so many other choices, then I can surmise a few things about you. You are a thoughtful, caring person who has an inquisitive soul. You are deeply spiritual, even if you don't attend a religious service. Even if you do, you feel that you want more, more meaning in life. Maybe you aren't sure what yet, but you are seeking *something*. You believe in causes and participate in activities that you hope will make the world a better place. You have moments of spiritual awareness that bring you great joy. Yet, these aren't frequent enough. You want to cultivate a more permanent, dependable connection with Spirit. Lately, you have been feeling the need to be connected to something deeper, and yet higher than yourself.

You are an active member of society, but you know the "rat race" isn't all there is to life. There is a spark of the Divine within you.

You want this spark to shine more brightly. You wonder if other people feel it too. Sometimes you look into other people's eyes, trying to find the Divine Spark within them. You want some way to talk about this with others. Some language that hasn't been invented yet. It's a spiritual language of the heart. Who else can speak it? Where can you go to talk about these things? You keep searching. Deep down you want to grow and nurture your spiritual life. You know that your Creator, however you define this, is seeking a deeper connection with you.

Meanwhile, you go about your day, every day, doing remarkably similar things. You work hard either in an unpaid position such as raising your family or a conventional career outside the home. Weekdays are hectic and sometimes weekends are even worse! You are a busy person who has many demands on your time. Your family and friends are your main priority. After accomplishing everything you must do in any given day, you barely have time for yourself. This is a sad, common theme in our society.

When you do have a few minutes to relax, what do you do? A lot of people sit on the couch and watch TV and have a snack. Now, I don't judge, in fact, I am the best couch-surfer there is! Yet, I want to give you an option that you might not have considered. It's something that can be done fairly quickly. In fact, in just one fraction of your downtime, you will feel more relaxed than after an hour of TV and snacks. You guessed it, it's called meditation.

Perhaps you already have a meditation practice. That's great! Just add my technique to what you are already doing. It will enhance your spiritual path in unbelievably beautiful ways. If you are just starting out, I am so happy for you! You are about to embark upon a new journey that will be full of love and miracles. At the very least, meditation is a great way to relax and find something deeper in your life.

I can hear you ask, "But, what is the best way for me to meditate? There are so many methods and I don't know which one will give me the maximum benefit. Later, I will give you an overview of the history of meditation and various techniques that have been popular. Then I will share my simple technique and let you decide what will work best for you. I really won't mind if another method is best for you. All I care about is that you, in your busy life, find some way of connecting more deeply to your spiritual self. Your True Self.

WHO AM I?

Just to inform you of where I am coming from, as your meditation teacher, it would be good for me to briefly discuss who I am and how this meditation technique came into being. I am not writing this so you will compare my spiritual development with your own, or with other teachers. Every person on the planet is equal and unique in their spiritual development. No one is better or worse than anyone else, deep down.

But for the sake of understanding why I came to write this book, please allow me to tell you a bit about myself. Currently I work for a large non-profit community network. We assist individuals who are dealing with issues of poverty and homelessness. Specifically, I help them find and keep good jobs. Also, I am an ordained Inter-Faith Minister, from One Spirit Interfaith Seminary in New York City. I also took a year of spiritual counseling classes there. I love to perform weddings, baby blessings, and even memorial services when needed. My paid work and my ministry are both important to me. This is my present moment. In the future I would like to be a full-time author, teacher and public speaker on integrated spirituality.

But where did I come from? You can skip this part if you want, but if you are still interested, let's go back to October of 1962. I was born at the height of the Cuban Missile Crisis. I always felt that I was sent here to Earth to tip the scales in favor of Peace.

I was surely blessed, being raised in a loving Christian family. We went to First Lutheran Church of the Reformation. This church is gorgeous, like a cathedral in Europe instead of downtown New Britain Connecticut. It was built by Swedish immigrants, my Ancestors. It continues to be a beacon of worship and service to the poor. Not only did we go every Sunday but for choir and other activities during the week. As I was growing up my parents were incredibly involved there. They helped impoverished people and

refugees to get a hand up not a hand-out. I
learned so much, watching them.

When I was about twelve it was time to take
Confirmation Classes. This was a huge step to
becoming an adult member of the church.
Before one can be "confirmed" one must take
two long years of religious instruction. These
classes were given by the two senior
ministers, who were fairly strait-laced, and
one Youth Minister. Reverend Wayne Gill
rode a motorcycle, played guitar, and taught
some Buddhist and Hindu principles mixed in
with Martin Luther's catechism. This was
about 1974 and he was the classic hippie
youth pastor. All the kids loved him!

One evening, he had all of us sit on the floor
and close our eyes and breathe deeply for a
few minutes. He brought us through a guided
meditation. At some point, my spirit was set
free and I went to "another place." I don't
really know where, but I was *gone*! I
remember an amazing sense of peace and
freedom, such as I had never known. In some

nebulous way, I felt the presence of supportive angels or heavenly host, as they say. I have no idea how long I was "out." All the other kids were getting up to have their snack. As if from far away, I heard one of them ask the pastor if I were asleep and should she wake me. He wisely said, "No, she will come back when she's ready." I have always loved him for that.

Later, I talked to him privately and told him what had happened. He said that was excellent and not to be scared. He gave me some breathing techniques and ideas for how to do the meditation on my own. I was hooked! I have been meditating every day since then. Even in times of trouble, I still feel that joy, peace, and freedom while meditating. That is why I want to share it with the world. We can all use a little peace and freedom, right?

Since age thirteen, I have studied many of the world's religions and spiritual traditions. This included their prayer and meditation practices. For months at a time, sometimes even for years, I have practiced many versions of Hindu traditions, such as yogic breathing, chanting, and using mantras. I have gone on spiritual retreats of all kinds, where different meditation techniques were taught. I had many wonderful moments, but as I got older, something didn't feel exactly right. I was like a square peg in a round hole. I was so busy trying to learn the technique correctly, that I didn't always feel centered in my heart, deep in my soul. I guess you could say I was distracted by a sort of performance anxiety. Other people seemed to reach an enlightened place using these methods, but I rarely did. Then I would feel a sort of spiritual jealousy, which I know, sounds silly.

I must be clear that I did learn a great deal from all the teachers I've known. In fact, I'd like to acknowledge one of my teachers, Sant Darshan Singh. He was the leader of the group called Science of Spirituality. His spiritual lineage goes back to the great Guru

Nanak. He was a beautiful poet who described spiritual states of ecstasy. Meeting him in person was even better. His meditation technique was basically to chant several holy names of God. I was blessed to go with him and several of his students on a brief tour of the Northeast.

One of my favorite books by him is "The Secret of Secrets." (2)   I will always be grateful to him and this entire community.

I started to notice that when I was meditating in his presence, I felt completely connected to a Higher Power. Yet, sometimes when I practiced at home alone things were not all I hoped they would be. During my twenties and into my early thirties I also tried various forms of Buddhist, Transcendental and then Mindfulness Meditation practices. Each of these had something special to show me and I learned a great deal from each one.

Now I am in my early thirties and live in Eugene, Oregon. I was devoted to my career and to my wonderful co-workers. One of them invited me to her synagogue, Temple Beth Israel. For about three years this welcoming community opened my heart to new ways of loving God. I was blessed to attend Shabbat Services and all Holy Days there. Rabbi Myron Kinberg was a brilliant, warm and compassionate teacher. I was also blessed that he met me for coffee sometimes. We talked for what seemed like hours. He shared with me the great stories and wisdom of the Jewish faith. Rabbi Myron Kinberg taught me so much and his name surely is a blessing. I will always appreciate the good people I fell in love with there.

At about thirty-seven years old I obtained a scholarship and got my master's degree in Special Education from the University of Oregon. I credit daily meditation for the ability to concentrate and graduate in only one year. I started teaching preschoolers who were on the Autism Spectrum. I came home feeling satisfied on one level, but downright bone-tired on another level. In the cold damp of the Northwest I suffered from bronchitis and every winter it got worse.

Spirituality, which had always been my bedrock, now felt like quicksand. For several reasons, I began to suffer from a profound inner confusion about who, if anyone, genuinely cared for me. It was almost as if someone who had been supportive and affectionate, who encouraged me to depend upon him, suddenly acted as if he barely knew me. My deepest insecurities rose to the surface. I did not know how to let people go gracefully. I behaved badly, out of fear and grief. This made me even more ashamed and alone.

By December of 1998, I felt abandoned by those I loved most. Yes, I had friends and family "back home" who loved me but they were light years away. I was not practicing gratitude for what I did have in my life. This brought me into a downward spiral. Although I kept praying, more out of habit more than real faith, my connection to God was slipping away. My spiritual wound was like a big black hole. Anything good in my life was being sucked into this dark darkness and disappeared.

Fierce competition for good jobs meant I could only find part-time work. The hacking cough and congestion I felt during this particularly horrible winter turned out to be walking pneumonia. I was so sick, I could barely work. This made me so poor that I often had to decide whether to get food or gas in my car. I could not take a breath without pain and I didn't have health insurance. I was all alone and every day I became more and more alone.

I kept trying to meditate, but nothing helped me anymore. I was too far gone. I was about to give up on everything, including my life. All I could do was half-heartedly take a half-breath. Nothing else mattered.

One day in mid-January of 1999 I was going through the motions of meditating, as usual. I couldn't get on the floor or in any kind of pose any more. I didn't even have the mental energy to chant mantras. I needed something to reach deep into my heart and help me reconnect to a Higher Power. I needed to calm down my rampant anxieties. Nothing I knew of, nothing I tried, was helping me. I was too sick to even get out of bed.

During a sort of attempt at meditation, I sighed and asked God a question - although I wasn't sure He was still there. I whispered, "God, I am too weak to even meditate. My life sucks and it's all my fault. Do I even deserve anything better than this? God, can *anything* help me now?" Then I just went silent, too exhausted. In a way this was good because I was completely humbled and completely ready for whatever God had to say.

Suddenly, I heard that "small, still voice" that the mystics talk about. It was deep, calm, and sweet. I felt a Divine Presence was finally stepping in to help me. This Loving Entity said "Well, it's about time you asked Me.

Yes, there is something that can help you. Try it now and see how it works. From now on when you meditate, give thanks and then say this… 'God, please show me what you want me to see and help me to be who you want me to be.' Then just listen for awhile, then give thanks again." This meditation technique was so reasonable and effortless that I had a tiny mustard seed of faith for the first time in a long time. I also received the further instructions, which I will share with you soon.

It is significant that the new meditation practice came to me during this, the worst period of my life. When I think about this day now, I am so grateful. I was given a tiny ray of hope. Later, I thought about what was given to me as a sort of spiritual formula. There is a sort of alchemy to becoming truly humble and asking God to show what He wants to show. Then add a dash of gratitude before and afterward. I wasn't sure it would help me, but I kept with it. I kept practicing this method daily, as if my life depended on it. Because at the time, it did.

I realized that I might die in my bed if I didn't get treatment for both pneumonia and major depression. Somehow, by God's grace, I got myself to the hospital. I still have no recollection of how I got there or anything. All I remember is that everyone there rallied around me. The doctors, nurses and social workers all helped me to get onto state health benefits and get the proper medical treatment. I started taking Cognitive Behavioral Therapy which helped me to sort out my emotional quagmire. This combined with my new meditation technique had me feeling a little bit healthier every day. Each day made a little more sense. Not a lot, but a little.

In just a few months, I could see the fog lift a little. I needed to move away from Oregon and make a fresh start. I put my resume on a national website with the idea of getting a teaching job near my wonderful friends and family in Connecticut. I was developing a conditional sense of trust that maybe God had a Divine Plan for me, even if I didn't know what it was yet.

Just as I was ready to settle down "back home" I got a call from Crownpoint New Mexico. An Elementary School Principal urgently needed a teacher for preschoolers with severe special needs. By September of 1999 I was living on the Navajo (Dine) Nation, on the Continental Divide. I forgot about my problems and cared more for the little children who needed me and their families. I not only threw myself into teaching the people but also learning from the people. While studying the Dine culture I met a Medicine Man who was a great Teacher/Healer.

I began to have mystical experiences that I won't bore you with here. I shared these things with the Medicine Man. He immediately organized a sweat lodge, specifically for my healing. I was even blessed to meet a few Code Talkers, heroes from World War II. All of the Dine people were so beautiful and welcoming to me. I felt included in a social and spiritual way. These things, combined with the clean, dry air healed my body and spirit. It was a magical time, but I still felt the need to be closer to my family and friends on the East Coast.

So, back home I got a good job with Head Start helping children with disabilities. I became an ordained Inter-Faith Minister from One Spirit Interfaith Seminary in 2005. Since then, my life revolves around helping people who deal with disabilities and/or poverty. Not that I am a saint, by any means. I fully enjoy my family, friends, music, dancing and little adventures. I credit my meditation practice for bringing all these good things and people into my life. I have been through tough times but I can honestly say that ever since January of 1999, I have never felt alone, afraid or abandoned, ever again. My life is truly blessed and it gets better every day!

None of this would be possible without my meditation technique. I will call it "my technique" but please keep in mind, that is in quotes. I have no doubt that this method did not come from me, but from a Higher Place.

I have a hard time calling it a technique or a method. It is more like a lotus flower, which blooms so beautifully at the surface of the pond, although its roots are deep in the murky mud at the bottom. In the Winter of 1999, my life was made up entirely of that murky mud. It was all dark sludge. Now, in the Autumn of 2020, this book is the lotus flower, which I offer you.

> *"I will love the light for it shows me the way,*
> *yet I will endure the darkness for it shows me the stars."*
> *~ Og Mandino ~*

1) Think about a dark or difficult time in your life and list some of the things that helped you.

2) What kind of support system or community do you have around you now? Who will be there for you when you need help?

3) Would it help for you to reach out to any other people or organizations for support? Do some research on this.

4) In what ways are you helping others, or being that support system for others?

5) List any adventures that you would like to have in life, such as your "bucket list."

6) Now take a few minutes to imagine
   yourself doing those fun and amazing
   things.

CHAPTER FOUR
A BRIEF HISTORY AND A DEFINITION OF MEDITATION

"Meditation is a process of lightening up, of trusting the basic goodness of what we have and who we are, and of realizing that any wisdom that exists, exists in what we already have. We can lead our life so as to become more awake to who we are and what we're doing rather than trying to improve or change or get rid of who we are or what we're doing. The key is to wake up, to become more alert, more inquisitive, and curious about ourselves."
~ Pema Chodron

Do you want to wake up? Are you curious about yourself? I believe you are, otherwise, you wouldn't be reading this book. Meditation can be rewarding and even fun, but it is NOT for the faint of heart. Self-exploration is only for those who are curious, brave, and soulful. Don't do it unless you really want to know the inner workings of your soul. Meditation is also for those who would like to become more curious, brave, and soulful. The rewards that a daily meditation practice can create in your life will be amazing. Meditation is a down-to-earth way to touch the stars!

This chapter will offer an extremely brief and admittedly limited review of the history and definition of meditation. There is no way to explore all the topics related to meditation without filling volumes and libraries. And, this is not meant to be a scholarly paper, so I will just give you an outline. More than anything, this chapter is simply for context and background. I will give a sense of what I've learned about meditation over the years. If something interests you feel free to pursue your research on the topic. Be careful, however! Once you start delving into this, you might not be able to stop! The subject of meditation is a bit like the rabbit hole in Alice in Wonderland. It is quite impossible to get to the end of it, but in the end, the trip is quite wonderful!

Let's start talking about what meditation is and what it is not. Meditation has historically been (but does not have to be) attached to religion. Especially in modern times meditation can be more like an openness toward mental exploration. Many people throughout history have entered what we might call meditation. For example, Greek philosophers discussed the need for every rational human being to learn how to think deeply. It is a very human thing to go into reverie and thinking deeply.

I propose that meditation, in one way or another, has been with humanity from the beginning. That means in every era throughout history meditation has been there, in some form or fashion. Western cultures still sometimes treat meditation like a fringe phenomenon, but it is nothing new. In broad terms, meditation is a *specific* way of thinking deeply.

When Anthropologists study indigenous cultures from around the world they invariably find several things in common. For example, someone in the tribe takes on the role of a Shaman or Wise Man/Woman. This person may also be called Healer, Seer, or whatever title they prefer. He or she is someone who has attained great knowledge and experience. This includes what they discover while in trance or meditation. Some use substances to help with this, but some don't. Either way, this Healing Person enters a deep state of focus and attention. When they come back from their journey, they have special knowledge. This information is used to guide and heal the people of the tribe.

Although there is no written history of this, there is every reason to believe that if indigenous cultures today have such a person, then tribes of ancient times probably also had such a person. It is logical to assume that before recorded history, some form of focused attention, AKA: meditation has been used. Our Ancestors were just as intelligent, if not more so in some ways than we are. They went into meditation to heal others and guide the tribe because the success of the whole tribe depended on it. They had a reverence for nature, in all things, that modern people would do well to emulate.

HISTORY OF MEDITATION

Moving forward in time, let's spin the time wheel to about 1500 BCE in India. Sacred Hindu texts such as the Vedas and Upanishad are being written down. For generations, meditation and yogic practices were passed down from Guru (Teacher) to their students. This was still a closed system, in that you needed to be accepted as a worthy student. Usually you were given a specific mantra and other meditation instructions directly from the teacher. This is a beautiful practice but one that most people in the West would not have direct experience with.

By the late 1880s world travel was becoming more accessible. People in Western cultures such as the U.K and the USA were fascinated with the exotic world of the East. Swami Vivekananda made a grand tour and spoke to many large groups, most notably at a world conference in Chicago. He was a disciple of the Indian mystic Ramakrishna. Other

Swami's and Gurus traveled to the West and gave presentations.

Let's jump to Boston in 1920. A beautiful and exotic looking young Guru named Paramahansa Yogananda arrives from India. He practiced what is called Kriya Yoga and he embarked on an extensive transcontinental speaking tour. He was the first Indian to be hosted at the White House in 1927. He settled in Los Angeles and is often considered to be the "Father of Yoga in the West." His book, Autobiography of a Yogi, published in 1946 has sold over four million copies. (2) Even then, most people in the West did not participate in yoga or any formal meditation practice. They considered it inextricably linked with Hinduism.

BUDDHISM

Getting back to our time machine, let's set the dial back to around 600 - 500 BC. We find ourselves in the beautiful gardens of Lumbini, in southern Nepal. A young prince is born named Siddhartha Guatama. He was born into the Hindu upper class and is pampered and shielded from any ugliness in the world. Then one day, he saw a human being, sick and frail, and it changed his life. While most people in his position would ignore it, or at best throw a few charitable coins around, he left his palace to find out what was the root cause of this suffering.

Siddhartha wandered for six years, practicing various forms of meditation, some were harsh and extreme. Then one day he sat down under a Bodhi tree and vowed to remain there in meditation until he understood how to relieve the suffering of the world. After forty-nine days, on a night lit up by the full moon in

May, he became enlightened. He understood that the origin of all suffering is, simplistically, desire. Now, I want to caution folks that this "desire" doesn't mean that wanting food, shelter, or a loving mate is wrong. In this setting, "desire" is speaking about an esoteric principle that would take an entire book to explain. Suffice to say that Siddhartha Guatama became known as The Buddha or Enlightened One. He spent the rest of his life teaching people from far and wide how to relieve human suffering. Meditation is a huge part of his teachings.

Buddhist meditation has different aspects and it is more like a crystal than a singular concrete wall. It has many nuances and variations. Think of Buddhism like a river, with other tributaries and sources, joining in and flowing out again. In addition to what most people consider mainstream Buddhism, there is also Zen Buddhism and Tantric

Buddhism, which are important and influential. Each of these forms has their own meditation practices and traditions. I won't go into these myriad forms of Buddhism, but there is a great deal of literature available if you wish to pursue this. Since then, millions of people have received great wisdom and peace of mind from Buddhist traditions and practices. One book to start with could be with author Ryuho Okawa's The Essence of Buddha: The Path to Enlightenment, (3)

For the sake of simplicity, I will focus on the historical context or background of Buddhist-based meditation. One practice is called Vipassana. Roughly translated it means, "insight" or awareness of what is happening, exactly as it happens. In this practice, we are encouraged to watch whatever comes into our minds without judgment and then gently let it go. Another practice is called Samatha, or "Tranquility" which brings the mind to a resting state and trains the mind to be at peace and not wander from thought to thought.

I found a nice website (https://thebuddhistcentre.com/exeter/four-kinds, April 3, 2017) that outlines the huge subject of meditation into four main types. The author, simply named Mokshini, (4) gives a good explanation. Please note that some aspects may be similar or may overlap with other aspects or other terms for describing the same thing. For now, just browse through these four types of practices without pegging any of them into square holes. Here is the summary, from the website:

"1. Concentrative: There is a body of practices whose aim is to still the mind, to gather us together when we are dispersed, to help us focus and be present when we are distracted and 'all over the place'. Mindfulness practices like the Mindfulness of Breathing are a classic practice for this aim.

2. Generative: this is the body of practices that help us grow and develop more of a quality that we wish to have more present in our life - kindness, generosity, rejoicing in others for example. The basis for these practices is that we can train ourselves to have more of these qualities - like building up a muscle through exercise. The Development of Loving Kindness (metta Bhavana) is a key practice here.

3. Receptive: This is a key skill to learn - to be completely open and able to turn towards our actual experience, beyond and below our layers of cultural conditioning that makes us blindly accept assumptions of 'how things are'. The practice here is what we call in Triratna Just Sitting

4. Reflective: learning to think - in a relaxed, focused, directed way, allowing us to go deeper and find our authentic and truly creative way of relating to the world - the ability to do this very much depends on some grounding in the above three skills."

That sums up everything in a nice little nutshell. The influence of all the many faces of Buddhist meditation cannot be overstated. It would take a lifetime, or perhaps many lifetimes, to understand it fully. I also feel it's important to remind everyone that Hindus and Buddhists are not the only ones who enter into meditative states of awareness.

The Jewish faith has a rich tradition of meditating upon Bible passages, Hebrew letters, or cosmic concepts such as "before the beginning." In the book Jewish Meditation: A Practical Guide, by Rabbi Aryeh Kaplan, (5) he discusses the importance of meditation in Judaism. He believes that meditation is not a new fad, but an ancient part of the Jewish faith. He makes the case that the synagogue and prayer liturgy was meant to bring about a meditative experience, and deep connection with G-d. The subject of Jewish meditation practices can be studied further by seeking out a Rabbi and asking to have a chat. Take them out for coffee if they have time, and if they are a warm and generous human being, like my beloved Rabbi Myron Kinberg, you will have an excellent chat. Or you can just read a good book or two on this subject. I prefer a nice chat.

While we are discussing meditation, we can't leave out the Christian faith. Christian saints often discussed their connection to God through meditation. Because the practices of meditation are more famously from the Hindu and Buddhist faith traditions, some Christians may think it goes against their Christian values. I strongly disagree. I believe Jesus did meditate. What do people think he was doing all that time in the desert? I also firmly believe Jesus would like us to meditate as well.

In Luke 17:20-21, the New Testament states: "Now when He was asked by the Pharisees when the kingdom of God would come, He answered them and said, 'The kingdom of God does not come with observation; nor will they say, 'See here!' or 'See there!' For indeed, the kingdom of God is within you.'" (6) I believe he was referring to meditation. I know this will be controversial for some but look within your heart. Those who can understand will understand. If you don't believe me, just try it for yourself!

When we go within, into a deep and reverential state of meditation, we will find the "light and the way." I believe this is a cornerstone of Christianity. Jesus Christ came here for everyone who is willing to hear his message. So, go within to hear it! My method of meditation certainly does not go against any Christian teachings, and in fact, I hope it will enhance your Christian faith, no matter your denomination.

Over time, Christians have evolved into various denominations, some of them emphasize meditation more than others. Significantly, the Quakers have beautiful worship services and meditation practices which provide a great deal of wisdom and comfort. Meditation is not weird or foreign at all.

Some people may not realize this, but Islam has a profound connection to meditation. In 610 AC, the Prophet Muhammed (Peace Be Upon His Name) was a businessman. He could not read or write, but he cared so much about his community that he went into a cave to meditate and pray for its future. The cave was on Mount Hira, near Mecca. It was here that the Angel Gabriel gave him an important message and forced him to recite this until he memorized it. Over the years he received more messages and shared these with his family, friends, and community. These sacred words became the Quran, which is revered by millions of good people all over the world. The power and beauty of the Divine message he received while in meditation can't be overstated. Furthermore, Sufism is a way of worshipping Allah, and their meditation practice includes sacred dancing or spinning, while beautiful music is played.

Let's jump ahead to a summary of a few modern teachers of meditation. By the 1950s, a few Hindu Swamis, Gurus and Buddhist teachers had come to the West to share their teachings. Some supposed "Yogis" traveled around the country displaying their various extreme physical abilities as a sort of freak show. This included tricks like laying on a bed of nails or putting their bodies into impossible postures. These people may have had some spiritual knowledge but for the most part, they did more harm than good to the public relations of meditation. Unfortunately, many Westerners still consider meditation to be exotic or odd. This sad because it is neither exotic nor odd.

However, a few excellent spiritual teachers were breaking through to the Western mind. One of them was an early meditation teacher of mine, Sant Darshan Singh Ji Maharaj. His spiritual lineage (of teacher and student) went all the way back to the great Guru Nanak. He happened to be of the Sikh faith, but he offered his teachings freely to people of all spiritual backgrounds. He was the founder and leader of Sawan Kirpal Ruhani Mission and the Science of Spirituality. When I met him in the early 1980s, I was deeply impressed by his high ethical standards and humble, peaceful nature. Since his passing in 1989, his devoted son Sant Rajinder Singh has carried on the work of spreading peace and meditation throughout the world.

No spiritual teacher of the modern age has been as popular as Maharishi Mahesh Yogi. In the early 1950s his teacher, commonly called Guru Dev, encouraged him to go to the West and teach people a meditation technique called Transcendental Meditation ® or TM. The book on TM was extremely popular. (7) This is based on the ancient Hindu system of initiation and reciting of mantras. This practice was taught to millions of people during the 1960s and 1970s. It was a big part of the newly forming "self-help" or "self-awareness" movement. The Beatles, especially George Harrison were students of TM. Then it began a system of "teaching the teachers" and the movement spread even faster. Thousands of people became more familiar with meditation, but some became disenchanted because of various financial dealings and ethical concerns. I don't make any claims about this, either way. In any case, TM is strongly attached to Hindu teachings and philosophy. Not all Westerners are drawn to the Hindu religion, although there is one aspect of it that has become commonplace.

Go to any city in the U.S., Canada, or Europe and you will find several gyms and spas teaching the wonderful practice of Yoga. Untold numbers of people practice it at home, too. This is a healthful thing and I am glad people enjoy it. The type of Yoga that is practiced for health and physical well-being features a system of poses or "asanas." It's called Hatha Yoga, with Yoga referring to the mind - body connection. Many infer this to also mean a deep connection with Supreme Entities. It is interesting that the physical type of Yoga is so popular and commonly practiced, while meditation is still coming into its own. Some people still feel meditation is "not for them" because they are not Hindu or Buddhist. Yet, their Yoga has an unbreakable bond to Hindu philosophy and the acquisition of deep meditative states. So, every time you do the "Warrior Pose" or "Downward Facing Dog" you are participating in the beautiful tradition of Hinduism. The Yoga that we know of is just one aspect, which includes meditation. It is all "union with God" in different forms.

During the 1970's most people in mainstream Western culture still looked down upon meditation as a fringe element, most suitable for hippies. Then the Mindfulness-Based Stress Reduction program (MBSR) was created in 1979 by Jon Kabat-Zinn. (9) He was an MIT trained molecular biologist. He worked with the Department of Medicine at the University of Massachusetts (UMASS) Medical Center to create a system of meditation that would not necessarily have any religious views attached to it. It was informed by Buddhist practices but was created to bring the benefits of meditation to everyone, regardless of faith or lack of it.

By 1982, Jon Kabat-Zinn had done excellent research on how the use of Mindfulness Meditation could help in the treatment of chronic pain and stress. His program ensured that anyone, of any faith (or lack thereof), could enjoy its benefits.   Since then, MBSR has been studied and practiced widely, by people of all faiths and walks of life. This is the form of meditation that I used for many years. This method has been researched thoroughly and found to be effective for many people.

I hope that this little bit of history will not bore you but will help you connect the dots. This information is meant to be the briefest of brief introductions. I highly encourage further research if you are interested in any of these practices, mentioned above. For simplicity's sake, you can think of Hinduism as the source material for Yoga, TM, and similar types of meditation. Buddhism is the source material for Vipassana, Samatha, and Mindfulness Meditation practices. It is important to note that there will be overlapping concepts or similarities between various formats or practices. Meditation does not occur in a vacuum but within the great river of humanity. Just as physical Yoga fills a real human need for health and well-being, *meditation* fills a real human need for peace and inner knowing.

We will end our brief history for now. You may still be craving some definition or description of what meditation looks like or feels like. I will give you just a few things to think about. Researchers Walsh and Shapiro (2006) said "Meditation refers to a family of self-regulation practices that focus on training attention and awareness in order to bring mental processes under greater voluntary control and thereby foster general mental well-being and development and/or specific capacities such as calm, clarity and concentration." (10)

In all methods of meditation, an aspect of focused attention is important. Another research team, Jeyning, et al. (1992) stated that meditation is "practiced for the purpose of attaining a subjective experience that is frequently described as very restful, silent, and of heightened alertness, often characterized as blissful." (11)

By way of background, here are some of the ways people have found to meditate. These techniques generally fall into two main categories. They can either be under the large umbrella of Hindu or Buddhist traditions or even born from more modern, non-religious practices. The first is called "focused attention" (FA) or concentrative meditation. The other is described as "open-monitoring" (OM) which is popularly called "Mindfulness Meditation."

In FA meditation the practitioner concentrates their attention upon a mantra, breathing technique, or an image. A mantra is a repeated word or phrase that helps the person to focus their attention. The person can also concentrate on a general emotion or feeling. For example, someone might focus on the feeling of "peace" or "loving-kindness."

Some methods of meditation attempt to cease all unwanted thoughts. For the most part, this state of consciousness usually requires many years of dedication to arduous daily practices. Obviously, you can try this if you are drawn to it. However, very few people have time to spend hours in meditation trying to get rid of all their thoughts. With our busy lives, we need a technique that can provide results in just a few minutes a day, not hours.

The second main type of meditation is called "open-monitoring" or OM. Practitioners simply watch or monitor their meditation experience without judgment. Learning how *not to react* is the trick here. You try to suspend the running dialogue that usually accompanies all your thoughts. This is not as easy as it sounds. This is one reason why I would like to share my simple method of meditation.

This technique is simple yet effective. It combines elements of both focused attention and open monitoring. It offers a way to keep bringing your attention back to the present moment. It also provides a gentle and easy way to view your thoughts without continual judgment. We will go over this technique soon.

For now, just know it is natural for human beings to "think deeply." And humanity has come up with countless ways to meditate, based on their beliefs and culture. People who meditate are not some counter-culture fringe elements. In fact, I would propose that people who meditate are smarter than most because they have found a way to reduce unhealthy stress and find inner peace. In 2015, Jon Kabat-Zinn so eloquently said, "When we speak of meditation, it is important for you to know that this is not some weird cryptic activity, as our popular culture might have it. It does not involve becoming some kind of zombie, vegetable, self-absorbed narcissist, navel gazer, "space cadet," cultist, devotee, mystic, or Eastern philosopher. Meditation is simply about being yourself and knowing something about who that is." (12)

Also, when it comes to picking the right practice for you, look at all your options. My technique might not work for you. It's the easiest and simplest that I know of, by far. However, I honestly believe that any technique that works for you is a good one. My main intention with this book is for you to feel inspired to try a meditation practice, of any kind.

In this community, you are completely supported as you experiment and learn. You are a valued member of this tribe, as we learn together. Meditation is a way to rise above our day to day problems. It is a vacation from the rat race. It is a respite from the barrage of constant thoughts and the often-painful judgment of those thoughts.

Meditation is a subjective experience. If you asked a hundred people what meditation is like for them, even if they practice the same exact technique, you would get one hundred different answers. That is why I am adamant that your experience is real and valid, even if it is completely different from another person's experience. There are no "star pupils" in this effort. Only stars, which you already are!

"Meditation is the only intentional, systematic human activity
which at bottom is about not trying to improve yourself or get anywhere else, but simply to realize where you already are."
~ Jon Kabat-Zinn
(Aug. 2015, Life, Mindfulness)

EXERCISE

1) Of all the types of meditation practices, mentioned here, which one appeals to you the most? Why?

2) Which type of practice does not appeal to you and why?

3) Here is a riddle or koan for you - meditation does not have to be taught, but it does have to be learned. How can that be?

4) Take a moment to close your eyes and think about the quotes that bookend this chapter. What feels most meaningful to you in these quotes, and why?

CHAPTER FIVE

HOW IS MEDITATION DIFFERENT FROM PRAYER?

> *"Prayer is when we talk to God.*
>
> *Meditation is when we listen."*
>
> *~ Anonymous*

This is an adage, but overall, I think it's is an excellent distinction. Prayer is a particularly important part of most religions. Like meditation, prayer has been an integral part of human existence since the beginning. Prayer is a great way to express all your wants and needs, hopes and fears, and feel that you have been heard and understood. This alone can be a great act of healing. True prayer can be as healing as anything else we know, anything else we can try.

There is a lot of healing and recovery to be found from following the Twelve Step programs. For example, to reiterate the Eleventh Step, we "sought through prayer and meditation to improve our conscious contact with God as we understood Him, praying only for knowledge of His will for us and the power to carry that out." (1)

Wow, that is huge! If you have reached this step, you have already come such a long way.

This is a miracle. I passionately believe the technique I share will develop your "conscious contact" with your Higher Power. I focus mainly on meditation in this book but feel it is important to also discuss the power of prayer. A prayer is an act of bringing our needs and wants into alignment with a power greater than ourselves.

Every type of prayer, from requesting things such as prosperity and healing, to prayers of thanks- giving and praise – all of these can be found in every religion under the sun. It is impossible to count all the prayers in the world. Mahatma Gandhi said, "prayer is the very soul and essence of religion, and therefore prayer must be the very core of the life of man." (2) Mahatma Gandhi, "Speech at Prayer Meeting, Sabarmati Ashram," Jan 17, 1930. It goes without saying that Gandhi meant that prayer is the core of the spiritual *woman,* too.

Prayer is a way of bridging that apparent gap between God or the Higher Order of the Universe and our small, transient bodies. For most of our day we go about our business believing that we are one thing, over here, and God is another thing, over there, somewhere. Prayer is a way of bringing the two together, any time that reminder is needed. That is why I deeply respect Muslims who pray five times a day. Prayer is a way of developing that relationship to our True Self and the Divine Creator. Prayer puts our mind at ease when we need it most. Prayers of thanksgiving assure God and ourselves that we are grateful to be alive.

Meditation is a different method of doing the same thing. Only instead of going outward from ourselves, with prayers going somewhere "out there" we are going inward. It is about shutting the heck up and just listening for a change! I say that to be a little funny, but honestly, at times it is so important to be in silence and listen to God. It is a way for mere mortals to learn from that Being or Force. Prayer is a way to tell a Supreme Entity all about your earthly troubles. Share everything happening in your daily life. You can ask for what you want. Then you can say "Thank You" for having received what you need. Even in times of our greatest crisis, when we think God has denied us what we want most, we can give thanks - because He has given us what we *need*. We might not like it or understand it, but a sense of gratitude will work miracles.

Some people have trouble with the period of time after a prayer of request is made and before they receive God's abundance. This gap can feel as big as the Grand Canyon! This is the sacred moment when people of faith are being asked to show their inner strength. We have to fill that (apparent) huge divide with the faith of the mustard seed, one of the tiniest seeds on earth. Imagine, you are at the Northern Rim of the Grand Canyon. You have asked God for something truly important, truly necessary. You have not received any signs or answers yet. Maybe it has been days or weeks or even years. All you can do is take out a tiny mustard seed, put all of your faith into it, and throw it into that awesome Divine space.

During that sacred moment it is vitally important to pray with thankfulness. Especially if we don't see literal results yet, saying prayers of thanks is so crucial. Developing that feeling of being rest assured that God is "on it" is a very high, noble practice. In between asking and getting, be thankful. We can pray with the faith that whatever it is we need most, we *are* about to receive it. As everyone knows, the final outcome of our prayers may look quite different than what we had hoped for. This is because we don't have the same perspective as God or the Universal Energy. If we did, we would always know that our prayers are answered in the best possible way, for us, at that particular time.

The best kind of prayer is to ask for understanding of the Higher Dimension, The Creator of All Things. Our prayers for greater understanding will *always* be answered. In fact, if we pray for wisdom *first,* as Solomon did, all other great things will come to us as well.

Prayer and meditation have equal parts to play in the life of a spiritual person. I propose that if you are not religious, but simply a deep-thinking person even you can pray. Send up your heartfelt gratitude toward the Life Force or Energy that brought you into being. Prayer brings you into greater alignment with It.

Between talking to God and listening to Him, there is a perfect balance. Giving and receiving, talking, and listening. Each one is profound, beautiful, and sweet. No matter your beliefs, you must find this balance for yourself.

This will be a good place to feature a few prayers from various spiritual traditions. These are offered in no particular order of importance. In my view there are no prayers that are better than others. Any effort to worship and connect with a Divine Energy is valid and important.

One of the oldest prayers is called the Gayatri mantra which is from the Rig Veda (iii, 62, 10) which was written down in Sanskrit about three thousand years ago. It is highly likely this prayer was chanted for many generations prior to being written. Like many beautiful ancient traditions, the prayer was chanted/sung.

Not only was the literal meaning of the words being important but also the sound itself of the prayer was an integral part of the meaning. The inflection and rhythm of this chanted prayer can't be underestimated. I like that this prayer also talks about meditation, specifically.

For now, I will give you an English translation, but please remember that all these sacred texts go well beyond the printed page.

> *"On the absolute reality and*
> *its planes,*
> *On that finest spiritual light,*
> *We meditate, as remover of*
> *obstacles*
> *That it may inspire and*
> *enlighten us."*

So beautiful! Similarly, profound, here is a
traditional Buddhist prayer.

I like the way it asks for "happiness" and also
"the causes of happiness." This is a brilliant

distinction. Many people chant this prayer over and over again in a meditative way. There are many translations and variations of this prayer. All versions are immensely powerful.

If all humans lived in this manner, we would all enjoy eternal peace. We would always feel the "sacred happiness" which has no sorrow. Now I would like to share one of my favorite prayers from Judaism.

Read this and tell me if you don't see some similarities to Buddhist teachings of non-violence.

When I walk through thy woods,

May my right foot and my left
foot

Be harmless to the little
creatures

That move in its grasses: as it is
said

By the mouth of thy prophet,

They shall not hurt nor destroy

In all my holy mountain.

- Rabbi Moshe Hakotun

Any discussion on prayer must contain prayers from various Native American traditions. This one[2] happens to be from the Lakota Nation.

Wakan Tanka, Great Mystery,
Teach me how to trust
My heart,
My mind,
My intuition,
My inner knowing,
The senses of my body,
The blessings of my spirit.
Teach me to trust these things
So that I may enter my Sacred Space
And love beyond my fear,
And thus, Walk in Balance
With the passing of each glorious Sun.

---

[2] http://www.sapphyr.net/natam/quotes-nativeamerican.htm. (5)

I invite you to read more about the various indigenous people all over the world and their beautiful prayers. As you read them, I hope you will become even more keenly aware that all faiths, and in fact all people from around the world, deserve utmost respect. Prayer shows the foundation of mankind. Prayer can bring peace to the whole world. As we appreciate each other on a deep level, where we are brothers and sister, peace will be our prayer. To that end, some of the most profound prayers of peace come from Islam. Muslims are sometimes judged by their most extremist factions. This is a huge injustice. It would be like judging all Christians by the Crusades or Inquisition. It's important to note that similar to the various developments in Christianity, Islam has different practices and traditions. For example, Sufism is a beautiful tradition, one that is rich with prayer and meditation. They are known for meditating to sacred music, while spinning in perfect harmony with God. They are also famous for their great poet Rumi[3]. Every one of his poems are prayers. I recommend you read them all. I offer just one taste of his sweet love of God.

Visit the sick, and you will heal yourself.
The ill person may be a Sufi master,
And your kindness will be repaid in
wisdom.
Even if the sick person is your enemy,
You will still benefit,
For kindness has the power to transform
Sworn enemies into firm friends.
And if there is no healing of bad feeling,
There certainly will be less ill will,
Because kindness is the greatest of all
balms.
~ Rumi

----

[3]https//www.shortpoems.org/poets/rumi/short_poems_rumi
(7)

Many poems are asking God for change, in ourselves and in the world. One of the best things to pray for is peace. For our purpose of discussing what Prayer is, I can find no better example than this one, from the holy book – the Qur'an.

Oh God, You Are Peace
Oh God,
You are peace.
From you comes peace,
To you returns peace.
Revive us with a salutation of peace,
And lead us to your abode of peace.
- Prophet Muhammad (Peace Be Upon His Name)

The following prayer shows in such depth how the human spirit is indeed One. Read it once and then ask yourself if it is a Christian poem or from the Islamic tradition. Then read it again, knowing that all our so-called divisions are an illusion.

God is the light
of the heavens and the earth.
The smile of God's light
is like a niche in which is a lamp,
the lamp in a globe of glass,
the globe of glass
as if it were a shining star,
lit from a blessed olive tree
neither of the East nor of the West,
its light nearly luminous
even if fire did not touch it.
Light upon light!

- The Qur'an (24:35)- al 'nuur - The Light

So many of these images remind me of Christian themes such as "the Light" and "the Way." There is a connection here. It never ceases to amaze me that when you study the religions of the world, *when you really get into the heart of them,* there will appear many more similarities than there are differences. I believe it is our human condition to pray. We all want to enter into a dialogue with something or someone who is beyond our mortal selves.

In two of the New Testament books of the Bible, attributed to Luke and Matthew, we are given the Lord's Prayer. (10) This prayer comes directly from Jesus Christ. I know there are many different versions and in fact, I enjoy the Aramaic version very much. But I

would like to share the version that I learned
in the Lutheran church as a child.

> Our Father who art in heaven,
> hallowed be thy name,
> thy kingdom come,
> thy will be done on earth as it is in
> heaven.
> Give us this day our daily bread;
> and forgive us our trespasses
> as we forgive those
> who trespass against us;
> and lead us not into temptation,
> but deliver us from evil.
> For thine is the kingdom
> and the power and the glory forever
> and ever. Amen

Let's analyze this prayer for a moment. Jesus is teaching us several things here. I am going to write a little stream of consciousness here so forgive my grammar. First and foremost, Jesus wants to help us to remember that our Father is in heaven and yes, His kingdom will come. Therefore, we should change our ways and do things on earth as they are done in heaven. This is a funny kind of prayer because it is not asking God to change but for us to change. Next, we are asking for a few things. We ask for our daily bread – we are not asking for enough bread for a week or a month. Just what we need for today. Equally important as surviving – that is, having enough food for the day is *forgiveness.* We need this as badly as food. Furthermore, we need to *give* this exact same forgiveness to others. Because they *need* it as badly as their daily food. To withhold it from them would be just as horrible as to starve them. Wow!

Next, Jesus has us pray for the strength to avoid temptation of any kind. Now, He knows that God does not tempt us to do bad things. But He is teaching us how to pray so that every day we will *remember* to avoid doing bad things. Those who know what is right and wrong, but do wrong things anyway, that is the evil he speaks of, in my opinion. I believe He was sharing again one of his deepest beliefs that hypocrisy is the worst. The people who act high and mighty in public but do terrible things in secret - Jesus always talked about them. So, I believe this part is warning us against the hypocrisy of the human heart. It is too bad that the self-righteous religious leaders (of any faith) who get caught up in terrible deeds, have not prayed this part a little harder.

Lastly, Jesus reminds us that despite any so-called evil in the world, God still is firmly in control of "the kingdom" and He has "the power and the glory forever and ever." This assures us and gives us that faith, each and every day. This prayer is a miracle itself. It brings the person who is praying into greater alignment with God. All prayers, from all spiritual traditions do this.

I think by now you can see the differences between prayer and meditation. When we meditate, we are sitting in silence, ready to receive whatever God or Universal Energy wants us to know. When we pray, we are asking for our daily physical needs and our spiritual needs to be met. We are asking for peace, forgiveness, love and healing. And, we are promising God that we will share this bounty with others. All these prayers are heavenly and provide much-needed encouragement in this world.

Even if you do not believe in a religion or personal Entity, prayer can open a dialogue between you and that Universal Energy which created you. Then hold in your mind all of the things that are important to you. This may be the need for better health for you or a family member, or prosperity in general or a wish for greater environmental protections. There is no topic that isn't okay to pray about. So when you think of these things you are concerned about, imagine you are surrounded by a sort of 5G network, or the highest level of communication possible. Speak from your heart to the Divine Spark. Plainly and simply. It will hear you. Then rest assured that the vast and awesome energy that created both the sun, the rivers and you will do whatever is good and right. You don't need to "push the river."

For example, here is a prayer I wrote for a friend who identifies himself as Agnostic and who has a chronic illness.

The Agnostic's Prayer for Healing
Dear Universal Energy,
You flow through the stars and rivers and mountains
And you flow through my heart, mind, spirit, and body.
I call on you now, wherever you are and whatever you are.
I have suffered in pain and I come to you now, a humble human, in need of comfort.
I know that the Spark of Energy that created the Universe
Has also created my spirit and my body.
I open myself to receive healing and greater alignment with Universal Energy.
Thank you for all that you have given me
And all that I will receive in Life.

This is just one example of how you can create your own prayer, no matter what you believe. Whatever your situation, don't be afraid to pray. Just make sure it is from your heart. Especially if you are in distress, pray from the center of your being. Don't worry about which words to use. Don't use the fanciest words you know. Sometimes when we are going through difficult experiences, we don't even have words. At that point, I recommend people pray by just crying out "GOD!" Your Creator knows what you are going through and exactly what is needed.

Make sure that no matter how sad or traumatic your experience, you reach up high for some type of gratitude, even if it is just for a second. I swear that this will not discount or negate your suffering. Believe me, it will do the exact opposite. Being grateful sets into motion positive energy that can snowball into wondrous and miraculous events. Similarly, showing gratitude for what you have, even if you still have pain or illness, will bring some measure of peace. A prayer that ends with gratitude has a mystical power that cannot be described in words.

As we have seen in this chapter, prayer is an active way to communicate with God or Universal Energy. It is like a telegraph signal that sends along a message, all the way down the line. The words are just dots and dashes that relay meaning. All your hopes and worries are fully understood, of that I have no doubt. It's a way to send out an SOS for healing or a new job or spiritual comfort. God already knows what you need, but the act of sending out a prayer can bring you into alignment with His Divine Will for you. Or the Universe's grand plan, however you view it.

Lastly, let's talk about the Serenity Prayer, which has been used so successfully by

millions of people from around the world. It
can help anyone, dealing with any problem.
It is a stroke of genius.

God grant me the serenity to accept
the things I cannot change,
The courage to change the things I can,
And the wisdom to know the
difference.

Prayer and meditation are like two sides of a
coin. Most people understand how to pray,
but not as many know how to meditate. They
are both so important. Meditation is about
sitting in silence and receiving information or
inspiration from God or Universal Energy.
Prayer is equally important, yet different in
the life of a spiritual seeker. We need to bring

this into a balance. Giving and receiving, talking, and listening.

When you pray, hold in your heart all of the things that are important to you and send these images toward the Force that created you. You don't have to get out a GPS and track the direction of the communication. It will go to the right place. Prayer is a vehicle for sending our deepest Truth directly to God or the Divine Spark. Meditation is when we sit in silence and listen for the answer.

> Prayer does not change God, but it changes him who prays
>
> ~ Soren Kierkegaard

EXERCISES:

1) Do you believe in prayer, if so, how do you pray?
2) How does it affect your life?
3) Close your eyes and say a silent prayer. If you don't believe in God, just speak whatever is in your heart. You can say something you're worried about, or thankful for, or both.
4) If you are praying for yourself or another person to be healed of mental, physical, or emotional distress – take a moment to see him or her (or yourself) in a perfect state of well-being. Use all your imagination skills to see this person as whole and complete. For just a minute, do not focus on their problems, but on their best self. What does he or she (or YOU) look like, act like, feel like, when at their best? Hold that image for as long as you can. Then give thanks for that vision, however brief it may have been.

CHAPTER SIX –

BENEFITS OF MEDITATION

Now we know a little more about the history of meditation and how it is different from prayer. Let's talk about some of the great things meditation can do for you. I want to remind everyone that this book is a love letter, not a research paper. It is based on my personal experiences, not research studies. However, if that interests you it's easy to do an internet search for "Research Studies on Meditation." You will find dozens of articles. There is a wealth of information and research studies for you to comb through. From there, you can begin your own exploration.

My intention here is to point you in the right direction. I want to carry on with the business of sharing my technique, or rather the method of meditation that was given to me when I needed it most. Maybe you are in a position where you need it too. So, we will stipulate to the fact that there are dozens of excellent research studies out there and you can enjoy them, as you wish.

My main point in this book is to relieve the suffering I feel in the world today. That is, I can sense the horrible stress that is plaguing the modern world. I am a humble person and not even close to the enlightenment of Buddha. But, like Him, I also feel the suffering of people. That is why I offer my simple meditation method as one way to alleviate some of the suffering.

PHYSICAL BENEFITS

Chronic stress is so rampant today that something must be done about it. Maybe we don't have to run from lions anymore, but we have to deal with stressful things that our Ancestors did not. We have traffic and complicated jobs and conflicted feelings about our family, community, and world events. The effects of being stressed become worse and worse over time. Some of us are in crisis because we are struggling with poverty or under other tremendous stress.

This can show up in physical ways. Maybe you feel the tension tighten up your neck, shoulders, or lower back. If you feel these things day after day, with no end in sight, it is only logical that a sense of "dis-ease" will begin to impact your life. Anything we can do to change our lifestyle and mitigate these effects would obviously have a positive impact on our physical health.

There is some scientific evidence that meditation helps people. In 2011 the Harvard Women's Health Watch published a study based on Mindfulness Meditation. The MRI images from the group that meditated a half hour a day were different from the control group who didn't. The areas of the brain affecting "introspection, empathy and the ability to acknowledge the viewpoints of others" seemed to be benefited. Meditation also appeared to positively affect areas of the brain that dealt with "fear, anxiety, and stress." It should be noted this was a small study but its suggestions are intriguing. It was further stated that "we already know that learning new physical skills (such as juggling) can change the brain." (2) So, why not meditation?

There was also an interesting article called "Meditation: A simple, fast way to reduce stress" was written by Mayo Clinic staff from the website https://www.mayoclinic.org,(3) it states, "if stress has you anxious, tense and worried, consider trying meditation. Spending even a few minutes in meditation can restore your calm and inner peace." It goes on to say "meditation has been practiced for thousands of years. Meditation originally was meant to help deepen understanding of the sacred and mystical forces of life. These days, meditation is commonly used for relaxation and stress reduction." In my method, meditation is for relaxation, stress reduction and to deepen our connection with the "mystical forces of life." As the Mayo Clinic article continues, "meditation is considered a type of mind-body complementary medicine. Meditation can produce a deep state of relaxation and tranquil mind."

Now, to be clear, these studies have informed my beliefs and are not conclusive. All I know is that a daily meditation practice can promote a sense of well-being. One might refer to this as a feeling of "ease." This is opposed to a state of "dis-ease." Meditation offers a way to mitigate the stress of modern life. Further changes might have to be made to reduce the long-term impact of a chronically stressful lifestyle. That is for each person to decide. Meditation is like taking a little hike to a pure spring and taking a fresh, cool drink. It might not cure everything, but it doesn't hurt, and it just might help – a lot!

Since before time, human beings were conditioned to deal with sudden bursts of stress, handle it, and then have a period of relaxation and restoration. We hunted or ran from animals hunting us. Then it was over and we dealt with it, better or worse. The stress did not continue non-stop every day, everywhere we went, all the time. Also, in ancient times we had our tribe to help shoulder the burdens of stressful situations. Unfortunately, in our modern world, our stress never seems to end. And our sense of a supportive tribe or community isn't as common. If we are lucky, we can lean on a supportive family and maybe our spiritual or neighborhood community. For the most part, modern people tend to deal with things on their own, which is a shame.

In years gone by it was more likely that we would have a small but reliable community that would help with everything from obtaining and cooking food to watching all the tribe's children. Life wasn't easy by any means, but people had each other. We tend to isolate ourselves now, with neighbors not even knowing their neighbors, never mind helping them bear the burdens of modern-day stress.

From the moment we wake up until the moment we lay down again, our lives are extremely fast-paced and stressful. This can cause you not to sleep well. Then you have a long and difficult commute to work. Most often, the actual workday is stressful. Then after a long day, already frustrated and tired, you are poorly equipped to handle the stress of the commute home. It's no wonder why road rage is rampant.

For those of you who work from home, you have your own daily stress. The kids get cranky, you get cranky. The washing machine breaks. The internet goes down just when you are about to start a web-meeting. Every day you must handle these stressful events. Every day there is more, not less. Unless you have a reliable source of support, the stress just keeps building up.

If you are like most people, you probably seek relief any way you can, usually in unhealthy ways. We all want immediate relief - fast and easy. It's easier to grab some comfort through instant gratification rather than taking a long-term, disciplined approach. Maybe you have a bit too much wine, or mac and cheese. Maybe chocolate. Or you indulge in various addictions. It happens to the best of us, believe me.

We know that in the long run, these things will not help with stress. Even while we are pouring that extra glass of wine, or whatever, we know there must be a better way. The problem is it takes a long time to make healthy daily habits. The best thing we can do is create a menu of stress relievers that we can depend on. If you always call a friend to debrief a stressful day and one day, she is busy, go right away to some other stress reliever. Get a massage, take a bubble bath, play with your kitty, or make yourself a great salad. Don't wait - if one thing doesn't work, choose another good thing. One thing that provides reliable and fast stress-reduction is meditation. Try it every day and see if your body becomes more relaxed.

EMOTIONAL BENEFITS

If you meditate every day you will start to notice many emotional benefits as well. Again, I am not speaking as a therapist. I have noticed that those who meditate report feeling more thoughtful in their reactions to difficult situations. They feel more resilient and able to adapt to change without freaking out. Meditation creates a small space, where the monkey-brain, the one who wants to throw poop, can take just a second to think about it first. Where an immediate reaction or overreaction once occurred, a little deep breath can happen instead. Then maybe a better solution than poop-throwing appears. That is the emotional benefit. Can't we all just agree to throw a little less poop at each other?

When you connect to your Creator or Universal Energy, you develop an awareness that you are never alone in this world. You will feel more love, and in return, you will be able to share that love with others. No matter what kind of terrible day you had, the next morning when you meditate, you start with a brand new, clean slate.

Throughout your day, you may notice that you aren't shaken off balance as easily as before. Even when confusing or negative things happen, you can bounce back quicker. It is just as important for your psyche to meditate as it is for your body to take a shower. Wash that stress and anger off you. Put on some moisturizer of love and peace to start your day. This will have a direct correlation with your newly calm attitude and this will result in more peaceful actions.

From my experience, daily meditation will help you gain clarity, focus, and attention. These things may translate into an improvement in your social and professional interactions. No matter what happens in your life, the daily trials and tribulations, meditations will help you to become more like a strongly built ship, able to sail through the vast oceans of life.

Of course, this is a life-long process. There will always be people who irritate us or drain our energy. This is the human condition. After you have been meditating for a while, you start to notice that those people don't affect you as much as they used to. You may find that they suddenly exit your life, or you don't have to deal with them as often. This is because when you tend to be more positively charged with good energy, those people who are negatively charged (with anger, frustration, for example) can't tolerate being around you as much. Or, at least they can't bother you as severely. For the most part, these are not "bad" people. They are just very good at finding your buttons and setting off your alarm bells. If you meditate eventually you will calm down all the alarm bells or at least make them a bit quieter.

Now, I'm not saying that your mother in law, for example, will just evaporate into the cosmos if you start to meditate. Sorry, no. However, I do suggest that if you meditate, she won't irritate you as badly. Probably she will sense that her negative comments don't "land" on your internal buttons the way they used to. Your calm reaction will not be as much fun for her. You no longer react in a way that encourages her to continue.

Your visits, while perhaps still necessary for family reasons, will be less stressful. This is because you have developed the ability to stop and fill your heart with only love and compassion, no matter what other people do - or do not do.

You will notice that not only are negative situations and people moving out of your life, but positive situations and people are moving into your life. With daily meditation, you are broadcasting to whatever powers that Be that you are ready to accept more good things. You have created more room for the good stuff so welcome it in! It is all here, just waiting in the wings for you. Daily meditation practice will get you ready for these new, wonderful changes. It will raise up your vibration and get you on an emotionally and physically uplifted state of awareness. Meditation will bring you into alignment with your True Self. You will feel more connected to your values of compassion and peace.

IMPROVES CREATIVITY

Meditation will also increase your inspiration and creativity. Even if you don't consider yourself artistic, you will find creative solutions to your problems. During meditation I received the inspiration for an entire series of novels called The Scandea Saga. I enjoy writing every day. I receive ideas for creative projects all the time. Whatever you like to do, from arts and crafts to composing symphonies, meditation will release a wellspring of creativity. You may get the impulse to try a brand-new creative outlet.

The specifics will be different for each person. I am sure that whatever you are into, whether it is crafting, singing, or being a good doctor or businessperson, your creativity will be enhanced by daily meditation. I am not unique in this. Einstein had what he called "thought experiments" that were a kind of meditation. This helped him come up with all kinds of amazing scientific theories.

ENHANCED SPIRITUAL DEVELOPMENT

Meditation has always helped people get in touch with their innate intuition. Some would say that the subconscious knows these things already. I won't try to describe how that works or put it in a box with a bow on top. I don't want to ruin the surprise for you.

I believe that our deeper selves can know things that our day-to-day selves don't recognize. Dreams and meditation can bring otherwise hidden things up to the surface. We can "learn" things from our depths that are helpful and important to our daily lives. In meditation you may suddenly realize a great opportunity on the horizon that you hadn't thought about before. Not consciously, anyway. These so-called "miracles" are available to us every day!

When we meditate, we enter a sacred space, a "heavenly" place if you will. We let go of the petty problems of the mundane world. In this special world, we become connected to the beauty of life. You may feel the presence of your most beloved Ancestors or spiritual teachers. Or your inspiration may be more practical, and you find the strength to make healthy lifestyle changes.

My meditation method can be added to every spiritual practice that you currently enjoy. In fact, if you dedicate yourself to a consistent, daily practice, you will go deeper into your current religion or faith more than you ever dreamed was possible. Even if you have meditated for a long time with another practice, I think you will find that my simple method opens up new worlds.

Whether you are new to meditation or been doing it for years, with this method, you will begin a new sacred journey. I am so excited for you! Not only will you reduce stress and whatever physical tensions you carry, but you will increase your emotional resilience, creativity, and connection to your True Self. This is truly a miracle. Get ready for it!

*"Touch your inner space, which is
nothingness, as silent and empty as
the sky;*

*it is your inner sky. Once you settle
down in your inner sky,*

*you have come home, and a great
maturity arises in your actions,*

*in your behavior. Then whatever
you do has grace in it.*

*Then whatever you do is poetry in
itself. You live poetry;*

*your walking becomes dancing,
your silence becomes music."*

~ Osho

EXERCISE:

Read this exercise all the way through to get a sense of what we will try today. Then close your eyes and take a few deep breaths in this manner:

1) Breathe in slowly and deeply through your nose until your belly rises and is full of healthful good air. Breath in, one, two, three. Keep breathing until the top portion of your lungs is filled to capacity. Then hold it for a second.
2) Let your breath come out through your mouth, like a deep sigh. Again, one, two, three. As you breathe out, imagine any stress or frustration you've been feeling simply is expelled. Just let it go - through your exhale.
3) Do this at least three times. With each breath, feel your neck, shoulders, and chest all relax. When you breathe in

again imagine that all good things in the universe are all around you, you are breathing in healing, positive energy. Exhale out any negativity you've been holding on to. Feel how much more relaxed you are with each deep, healing breath.

Now just let your mind wander for a few minutes.

Imagine your brain is churning out thoughts just like products such as candy, that is being made in a big factory. Swirling random thoughts are combined from various ingredients into a huge industrial mixer. Then they come out of the mixer and are poured into molds of various shapes. The mixture cools and solidifies. These shapes (your thoughts) come down a long conveyer belt Imagine that you are the Quality Control person. You stand and judge each thought as it comes down the conveyer belt. This has been your job for so many years. Well today, you can take a five-minute break. For just five minutes (or longer if you have time) it is okay to just walk away from that conveyer belt. You can let the thoughts come through as usual, but you don't have to stand and judge them.

 No, you're not going to be in trouble for this. You have been given permission to walk away for a few minutes. So, for now, let each thought go past and down and away and off into the distance. You don't need to know where they are going or to pick any of them up. They are going exactly where they need to go. Everything is fine. Whatever comes down that mental conveyer belt is fine. Enjoy your five-minute break.

If the "Thought-factory" image doesn't work for you, try this. Imagine your constant stream of thoughts is like a big river. It comes down from a beautiful mountain. Then it comes around a bend, and through the forest and the field. Eventually, this river of thought comes to a place where you stand, on the bank of the river. A big waterwheel is on this river of thought. You watch in pleasant amusement as all your thoughts come along, go up into the water wheel, make it turn, make a little splash, and then they go back into the river. Watch as your thoughts simply float away, downstream. There is no need to change the course of the water, or to do anything. Nothing you need to do but observe. You don't need to record or judge your thoughts. Just let them come down, into the waterwheel and back downstream. Simply rest on the grassy riverbank and observe your thoughts without judgement. There is no right or wrong. Jot down any observations that came up for you.

CHAPTER SEVEN:

SETTING THE SCENE FOR MEDITATION

AND A WORD ABOUT THE THIRD EYE

*"When the doors of perception are cleansed,
we see everything as it is, infinite."
~ William Blake*

If you have been reading this book in the manner I suggest, which is one chapter a day, then you have already started to develop your meditation practice. You are closer than you think to a reliable way to reduce stress and increase your creativity and spirituality. This chapter will outline some theoretical and practical ways to set up your daily meditation practice.

DON'T HAVE EXPECTATIONS BUT SET GOOD INTENTIONS

The first thing you need to do is set your intentions. Why are you doing this? It's particularly important to write this down, either in a separate journal or here in this book. You are going to encounter distractions, rebellion, and mental push-back. When your intention is clear, you will eventually get through all of that. Remember that every moment that you spend in meditation will pay rich rewards.

So, be resolved to try it for thirty days. If it doesn't help you, so be it. But for that month, make a commitment. Carve out time each day. As the title of the book promises, it can literally be just five minutes, to start.

Just as you brush your teeth, make this one of your "must-do" activities.

ELIMINATING DISTRACTIONS AND CARVING OUT TIME

Choose a time and place where you will have the fewest distractions. Many people like meditating early in the morning before anyone else is up. This works for some people but won't work for everyone. There is nothing wrong with taking time during the middle of the day.

And other folks like to meditate at night before they go to bed. This is tricky because you might just fall asleep instead of meditating.

Take a few days to experiment with the time and place. See what fits best into your lifestyle. However, once you get into a pattern that works for you, keep to that schedule as best you can. Try not to go back and forth too much. Don't say, "Oh, well this morning I'm running late, so I will meditate later tonight."

This doesn't work. Commit to a time and place. It is an esoteric thing but there is a certain energy that builds up to support you when you prioritize something in your life, and you set aside special time for it. Then God or the Universe, or whatever you believe in will take notice. Exactly how you are rewarded will be different for each person, but I can guarantee you will be rewarded for your consistent effort in some way. The main thing is to set your intentions and stick to them.

This brings me to an important point: decide what you want from your new practice. Do you want to reduce stress? Develop more self-awareness? Become closer to your Creator? Write it down. Believe that it will happen, in some way shape, or form. Just remember that meditation is not like a genie in a bottle. You don't rub the lamp and get whatever you want.

It isn't about *getting things*; it's about *experiencing things*. It's all about the sacred journey.

We do not yet know which way our path will twist and turn through the forest of life. Meditation simply puts a bright light on the path. It helps you see your way. No matter how complicated or dark things may seem in life, meditation is a guiding light. Therefore, set your intentions, and light your way.

GET THE PEOPLE YOU LOVE ON BOARD

No matter what time and place you choose, there will always be distractions. Most of the time, these distractions come in the form of people. The people we love can suddenly need us for something as soon as we sit down to meditate.

It never fails, when we start to meditate the children will fight or need a glass of water or a big hug. Or we get an important phone call. These things could happen at any time of the day, but for some reason, they always seem to happen when we try to meditate. It is almost as if people feel a shift in energy and whether they are conscious of it or not, they want to be a part of it. Or they don't understand what you are trying to do and how important it is to you. Before you meditate and well before they interrupt you, take a few moments to explain your good intentions and why you are making this lifestyle change.

If you explain the benefits, especially the reduction of stress, most people will understand. Or you can assure them that by deepening your connecting to God you will become a kinder and more compassionate person.

Whatever your intention is for meditation, most of your loved ones will respect it. Let them know the brief period when you will meditate is special and please don't disturb. I sometimes explained that for me, meditation was like going to church or synagogue.

It is something just as sacred. They wouldn't call me there, would they? No, almost everyone understands the sanctity of this. If you keep gentle, but firm boundaries about this, it will all work out. Convince your friends and family that meditation is one of the best things you can do for yourself. If your children are old enough, invite them to try it with you. Any kid over ten can probably do this. Or, if your partner is open to it, you can meditate together.

Some people will applaud your efforts to meditate. Most people want to support you in living your best life. Assure those you love that they don't need to do anything but give you the time and space you need. Tell them this is a special gift that they can give you. Mostly, people wanted to know that you still love them and that you will always be there for them.

Sometimes our family and friends need extra time and support. So, if you know a loved one is going through a hard time, call him the night before your morning meditation. This way, you won't be distracted and worried about him and he is less likely to interrupt your meditation time. Then, call him again later in the day, if needed. It just takes a little thoughtfulness. There will always be difficult people in our lives and there is not much we can do to change them.

A few people will see you doing something good for yourself and this can bring up resistance within them. They may tease you about it, or act like meditation is something weird or silly. Don't believe them. They may even say snarky things like "are you done with your trance?" or, "have you attained enlightenment yet?" Ignore that stuff. That is their issue, not yours. You can only change your own behavior. If anyone has problems with this, keep setting clear boundaries and stick to them.

Here are a few more tips and hints. Whatever you do, DO NOT look at your phone, or check your email before you meditate. Don't watch the news or listen to your morning radio show first. Not even the weather. Turn everything off. If you have pets who always jump up on you, put them outside or in another room. Give them some special treats to keep them happy for a while.

Wake up a few minutes early when everyone is still asleep. This is what I do. I get up earlier than needed, have a half cup of coffee and a small bite to eat. This way, my tummy isn't grumbling, and I feel not the sleepiness of night. This works well for me, but you can try out various things that work for you.

THE FIRST STEP IS TO GET COMFY

Surprisingly, this is an important first step to the meditation method that I am teaching you.

Simply find a quiet place and get comfortable. You do not have to force the entire household into absolute silence. Meditation does not have to include uncomfortable poses or sitting cross-legged on the floor. You may have tried some of these methods and got frustrated. I have certainly tried different practices for years. Some of them required keeping my hands in a certain way or sitting in a lotus position on the floor. I spent a lot of mental energy reminding myself of the correct way to do it. Then after ten or twenty minutes, my legs would get numb and it was impossible to concentrate on anything spiritual. Many people love these meditation techniques and get a lot from them. If they work for you, I wish you all the best!

My method will not require any special poses, so get cozy. This will be different for each person. You can put a light blanket over you if you want, but it is not necessary. Find any position that requires no effort on your part to maintain. Some people like to sit on a straight-backed chair, with their feet firmly on the ground and their hands laying loosely in their lap. Or sit on a large pillow on the floor with your legs in front of you or crossed in a relaxed way. You can lean your back against a wall if you prefer. Whatever position you choose, make sure you can maintain it with a minimum of effort. I use a recliner chair. I put my feet up and I feel perfectly supported in this way for as long as I want. I don't feel any need to adjust my position.

It is also okay to lie down, such as flat on your back on the floor. However, it's best to choose a place *different* from where you sleep. Your bed has the specific intention of helping you rest and sleep, so don't mess with that.

Although dreaming can feel similar to meditation in some ways, they are definitely not the same. The consciousness for meditation has a much different energy from sleeping. They serve different purposes in our lives. So, don't lay down in a place where you will fall asleep. Any other position is fine.

I'd also like to talk about how to develop the right frame of mind. The beginner's mind is a real thing and it is very precious. Right now, you are just beginning a new practice. Enjoy this feeling to the fullest. Don't try to rush out of this phase.

It is important to let in new experiences, with a completely open mind. In meditation, you want to develop a feeling like when you are traveling to a new place. You are fully awake and ready to receive new information. You have a welcome curiosity, such as "Oh, there might be something interesting, just around the corner!"

The main thing to remember is that you are setting up a special meeting with your Creator, Or Universal Energy. Make it work for you.

STEP TWO – TAKE A FEW "CLEANSING BREATHS"

In my method, there isn't exactly a specific breathing technique that you have to maintain throughout the meditation. When we begin each session, we do start with some deep, full breaths. I will call this type of breathing "Cleansing Breaths." We brought this up during the last exercise. I will give you a quick reminder.

Breathe in slowly through your nose, using the count of three. Fill up your belly first, then the middle of your chest. Lastly, fill up the top of your lungs. Then hold the breath for a second.

When you let your breath out, let it out like a deep sigh. Just "Ahhhhhhh!" Also do this at the count of three. With each exhale of breath feel your shoulders and neck relax a little bit more each time. Enjoy a few more cleansing breaths. Peacefulness comes IN, the worry goes OUT. Love comes in anger out.

When you breathe in, imagine that you are bringing in all good things into your life. As you exhale, imagine that anything unpleasant, negative, or unwanted simply floats out of you and goes far, far away.

Inhale Happiness, love, and positive energy. Exhale any negative energy. It simply evaporates. When you are done, just sit in this beautiful moment. Even if you aren't quite "there" or relaxed yet, enjoy the relative peace that you do feel.

During our meditation exercise later, you will take just three or four Cleansing Breaths, then you will just breathe normally. Before we go into that, let's talk about the third eye.

STEP THREE – "DEVELOPING GRATITUDE"

The other thing you must do in my method is to develop a feeling of gratitude. From now on, we will start and end each daily meditation with gratitude. This especially important step is called "Developing Gratitude." Yes, you probably have difficulties and problems in life. I am not trying to discount that or minimize your hardships. But just before you start each meditation and when you are finished, take a moment to think of all the things that are going well in your life. Each little thing is so special. It may be hard to come up with a list of good things at first. Let me help to get you started.

No matter who you are or how bad things seem, you have people and resources of some kind. They might not be in your presence right now, but they are on the other end of the phone. Even if it is an AA hotline or other support network, those people are here to support your journey on Earth. If you run out of things to be grateful for, think about the big picture.

Have you had enough food lately? Are you relatively healthy? Even if you're not, aren't there some aspects of life that give you satisfaction?

Dig deep for gratitude if you must. At the very least, you are alive right now, during interesting times. Do you live in a country where you have at least some measure of freedom? Are you able to get outside or look out a window and see a flower? Or watch the snowfall? We all have a million things to be grateful for. Practicing this feeling is integral to the meditation technique I will share with you soon.

If you believe that you have nothing to be grateful for today, I've got news for you. Tomorrow you will have less. If you feel grateful today, tomorrow you will have even more.

INTRODUCTION TO THE THIRD EYE

I will stop with the "steps" of the technique for now to discuss another important aspect of this meditation process. This information will be used briefly in the exercise at the end of this chapter. So, let's discuss the "third eye" because it is crucial to this meditation practice.

The third eye is a spiritual doorway or gateway to higher realms of consciousness. Some people believe this is a fictional or imaginary thing, but I believe it is completely real. In my experience, the third eye is literally the "Door of Perception" that was discussed by luminaries such as William

Blake and Jim Morrison and The Doors. This third eye can "see" things that the two physical eyes can't see.

Let's begin with where the third eye resides. Some people already know this information, so forgive me and skip ahead if you like.

Basically, the third eye is between your eyebrows, but I want to be more specific about this because it will be important later. To find your third eye, draw an imaginary line from one eyebrow to the other. Now find the middle point. Going straight up from here, draw another line upward for about an inch and a half. Then, from the middle of the eyebrow point draw another line directly down to the beginning of your nose. Put little dots at the end of each line. Now, in your imagination, connect the dots. This makes an elongated diamond shape. You can round this out to be an oval shape if you wish. Lastly, imagine that this area is not on the surface of your skin, but just a little bit deeper into your forehead. I will be referring to this entire area as the third eye. In my method, when you close your eyes in meditation, you will always focus on this area.

At first, most people will only "see" a flat dark color. Brown, navy, dark gray, or black. This is normal. After some time and practice, you will begin to see nebulous shapes or a few bright spots of color in this area. Don't be distracted by anything you might "see" outside of this area. Keep your focus centered upon the third eye. This will eventually awaken your inner awareness.

Some folks may sense a slight tingling sensation here and this is perfectly fine. And it is also fine if you don't feel or see anything at first. It can take weeks or months to notice anything. The power of the third eye is that it opens up a new awareness and newfound wonder of being alive.

I will leave it there, for now, because through daily experience you will have your own doors of perception cleansed. It will be different for each person. For now, you have learned three steps of a seven-step process. So far, they are: 1) Get Comfy 2) Cleansing Breaths and 3) Develop Gratitude. In the exercise today we will concentrate on these three and I will teach you the others in later chapters.

 Consider this your invitation to leave your daily worries behind and enter into a "circle of love."

"Come out of the circle of time
and into the circle of love."
~ Rumi

EXERCISE:

Today's exercise will be the starting point of what we will do every day from now on. I will be giving you the first half of the meditation technique. In the next chapter, we will bring it all together.

Step One – Get Cozy. Find your special place of meditation, or "circle of love."

Step Two – Cleansing Breaths. Close your eyes and breathe deeply as we described earlier, three times.

Step Three - "Develop Gratitude." Think of all the things you are grateful for, such as your friends, family, home, work, and hobbies. Add as many things as you can think of – until you really feel how blessed you truly are!

Keep going until you fully sense gratitude in your heart. Feel your heart gently warm up with thankfulness.

Now remembering where the third eye is, concentrate your full awareness there. It is okay to imagine an elongated diamond, or a rounded oval, as you prefer. With your eyes closed, "look" into this area with a relaxed consciousness or curiosity. I call this the "Observation Zone."

If the idea of a bland shape doesn't appeal to you, try this. Imagine you are in a softly lit library full of wonderful old books. You are browsing around and then you notice something. There is a dark heavy wooden door several yards straight ahead of you. As you concentrate on this door you see a round opaque glass peephole in the middle of the door, inset into the top half. It is fascinating and enticing. Imagine you are walking slowly toward that door. Keep a gentle focus on that peephole in front of you. You don't have to understand it, but simply have faith that this third eye area is a sort of doorway.

Stay in your "Observation Zone" for five minutes or how much time you have. Look - without judgment - at everything that may come up into your "field of vision." Know that there is no need to question, pursue, or even comprehend anything that comes up. Just let it be - whatever it is.

Remember the "Water Wheel" image we explored earlier? You can use that idea to deal with any images that may come up for you now. As things pop up, let them flow away again. There is no way to do this "wrong." There is no one that you need to compare yourself to and this is not a test. Enjoy this time of relaxation.

At the end of five minutes, go back to the feeling of gratitude. Review the good things in your life. At the very least, give thanks for these few minutes of peace and relaxation. Thank yourself for giving this gift to your True Self.

Then when you are done, jot down everything that you saw, even if it is vague or simple. For example, you might write "mostly brown, but a few yellow dots," or, "spiral shape of light blue." If the image of a person pops up, write it down. Then, if you think they need a call, call them. This is all perfectly okay.

What you may see or not see is not important right now. Identifying where the third eye is and learning how it is a gateway – this is all that matters right now. Really get curious about it. What did you see there?

Some people, especially musicians may also hear tones or music. Make a note of this, pardon the pun! Whatever you noticed during the observation zone, write it down. This is all simple stuff and there is no right or wrong. You can feel good about yourself for successfully learning the first half of the meditation technique.

CHAPTER EIGHT: THE TECHNIQUE

I want to know how God created this world.
I am not interested in this or that phenomenon, in the spectrum of this or that element. I want to know his thoughts. The rest are details.
~ Albert Einstein

This meditation technique is like a "spiritual formula." It is specific, in its own way. I want to remind you again that I did not "invent" this out of thin air. At my lowest point in life I humbly asked God for a way to help me. I needed to bring my life into alignment with His Divine Will. It is important to note that in some mystical way, I was given this meditation technique. It was the Creator's way of healing the spiritual suffering that I was going through. It has sustained me and helped me create a life that is more in keeping with all the goodness God wants for me.

I know that no matter what you are going through, God wants good things for you too. He wants you to experience more wonder and joy and yes, True Love in your life. This technique is literally a step by step way to help you achieve this great goal – the goal of accepting unconditional love.

We have gone over the first few steps of this spiritual formula. Step One was to "Get Comfy." That is, choose a quiet, comfortable in a spot where you can meditate. Step Two was to take three "Cleansing Breaths." Then step three was to "Develop Gratitude." This is a critical part of the meditation, so I'd like to go into this a little deeper.

Aside from giving thanks for your family, friends, home, and job, another thing you can be grateful for is that God, Allah, or Universal Energy wants to spend time with you. Yes, *you*. Right here, right now. You are about to enjoy some precious time with your Higher Power. But as powerful as this energy is, you still must invite He/She/It into your life.

This brings us to Step Four, or "The Divine Invitation." This step means you are calling in God, Goddess, Allah, or Universal Energy. In whatever way feels right to you, mentally invite God, as you understand Him, into the room with you. Do this with complete humility, because yes, you are a cool person. But you are still a frail little thing, clinging to a rock, that is spinning through space, in an infinite universe. Almost unbelievably, God wants to talk to you. Really feel that. Feel the miracle of that. Be humble about that.

I will say from experience that it is much easier to be humble when you are going through tough times. Humility creates a Divine Opening of the Spirit. Or a yearning if you will. Whatever you are going through, bring it to meditation. For just a few minutes, hand your problems over to God. Or let the Universal Energy handle them for a while.

Give yourself a mini-vacation from your worries. Even if they are severe, God can handle them. You no longer need to question the details. God knows exactly how to comfort and support you through any issue or problem that any human being has had, since the beginning of time.

Yet, you still need to invite Him or Her in. This "Divine Invitation" may seem unfamiliar at first, but once you get the hang of it, you will feel the benefits. The main thing is to be humble enough to ask God to come in and sit down for a while.

Now I will give you Step Four of the meditation process. This is called the "Divine Invitation" that we just described. It is extremely important. I will offer you a way to do invite God or Universal Energy into your meditation. To start, gather up all the humility, receptiveness, reverence, and curiosity that you can muster. Then silently say the following:

> *"God, please show me what You want me to see,*
> *and help me be who You want me to be."*

Then sit in silence and look into the space of your third eye. This is Step Five. I call it the "Observation Zone." You will be observing without attachment or judgement everything that comes into the area of your third eye. Simply look and listen. Allow for the silence.

Let this sacred space be exactly what it wants to be. Don't try to make anything happen. Don't expect anything to happen. Let go of all that, for just a few minutes. Let go of any preconceived ideas about what is a "successful" meditation and what is not. If you find yourself dwelling on something you see, feel, or hear, simply stop. Take a deep Cleansing Breath if you want to and then repeat the "Divine Invitation." Do this as many times as necessary and feel no frustration with yourself. It is all part of the process.

When you begin to meditate, your mind will probably go into overdrive. You will feel extremely bored. Your mind might start acting like a little child that demands attention. Don't try to ignore your thoughts or push them away. Put your thoughts, like a child, into a loving embrace. Usually, when you hug a child-like that the first thing they want to do is run away and play again. So, treat your thoughts in the same way. Hug them and then let them go. Forcing yourself to stop thinking about something is the best way to keep that thought going. So, if you find that your mind has gone into hyperdrive, just accept it and just say the "Divine Invitation" again, silently, and reverently. This "Divine Invitation" will open up a dialogue of profound proportions.

*"God, please show me what You
want me to see,
and help me to be who You want me
to be."*

Then silently and calmly observe again - whatever you may see, think, and feel. Stay only in the area of the third eye, or "Observation Zone." We can call this Step Five. In this step, don't try to hold onto anything in particular. Just see it, and let it go. If some image won't stop popping up, you can ask, "Why am I being shown this right now?" Then silently listen or watch for an answer. If one doesn't come, let it go.

Let me break this spiritual formula down into its components. You are humbly inviting God or Higher Power, to show you *anything* that He/She/It feels is important – at this moment – for you to see. You are willing to remain open because you have no idea what God will show you.

This willingness to remain open is the miracle. And it won't be easy to maintain that miracle. So, when your mind goes astray, and it will, gently come back to the "Divine Invitation." Silently say it again, even if it is a hundred times. Please don't use it like a mantra however and chant it. That isn't what is going on here. It's just an invitation and an awareness that you are spiritually willing. It's the feeling behind the words. So, say it again if you feel the need, then sit in silence again. There is no shame to how many times you repeat it. Just make sure there is plenty of space in between each time you say it.

The part of this formula is so important. When you say this phrase, you are humbling yourself, in a good way. You are admitting once again that maybe you aren't always the best version of yourself that you can be. You are asking God to correct any failings on your part by revealing them to you.

You are asking for the strength and courage to correct those shortcomings. You are asking God to do *whatever it takes* to help you become a better person. Humility gets a bad rap in our modern society. That's too bad because it is a cornerstone of real spiritual growth.

Knowing that you are not currently perfect takes a tremendous amount of courage! I just want to take a moment a applaud all of you for your inner strength and willingness to "be who God wants you to be."

As you meditate daily, new things will be revealed, and you will indeed become exactly who God wants you to be. You don't exactly and specifically know who your True Self is yet, no one but the greatest masters do. Yet, have faith because with this spiritual formula, all will be revealed in time.

This journey isn't easy, but it will be beautiful. It is as if you are beginning an ascent of a beautiful mountain. You will have gorgeous vistas and many difficulties along the path. Yes, your footing will slip at times. But after a while, you will reach unbelievable heights of self-awareness.

No, you won't become perfect. Yet, you will become a perfect version of YOU. This is something you can be enormously proud of, that you are willing to climb this awesome mountain in life. And instead of literally having to climb up a huge mountain, all you have to do is sit there! How hard can it be to relax and observe whatever comes up in your third eye area. Not that hard, but not always easy, either.

Stay in Step Five, or the "Observation Zone" for as long as you can. As the title of the book suggests, even five minutes will be rewarding. At the end of this third eye observation time, there is another important step.

Step Six is called "Show Gratitude Again." Before you go on to the rest of your day, it is so important to thank God or Higher Power for your time together. Again, this is done with reverent humility. This can be a quick, silent "Thank You" or it can be a whole prayer of thanks. That part is up to you. However, expressing gratitude is essential to this meditation practice.

After that, you can wiggle your hands and toes or whatever way you wish to come back into your regular daily life. The last step, the Step Seven is to "Document." Just write down anything that you felt or observed, at any point during the meditation. You might notice that if you move your position slightly you felt more comfortable. Make a note of it. Or, you may have "seen" colors in your "Observation Zone." Or heard a high-pitched tone or music. Write down anything like that. You can also write things such as "felt like a damn fool!" It is all okay. Write down how your day went later on, or if you slept better after meditating, or whatever happened in your case. Try to do this every time. You might not notice progress but one day, when you go over earlier entries, you will be amazed at your spiritual progress. So that concludes the Steps of the Spiritual Formula or meditation technique.

That is literally all there is to it! It is so simple that you would hardly believe how effective it can be. This simple method will provide you with everything you need to relax and reconnect with your Creator. You will find that simplicity is the hidden treasure. It was a miracle in my life, but I had to ask for this, first. I had tried everything from my own limited human perspective and nothing worked. This "Divine Invitation" speaks to something deep within me. I do want to see what God has to show me. I do want to be the person God wants me to be. It is so real and down to earth. These words were not hard to remember or foreign. *This was me.* I was being real with myself, finally. Even now, I see new things and I grow as a person. I know you will too.

Gratitude, both before and after the meditation is key. When I learned how to feel a little bit of gratitude, although I had little goodness in my life, little by little more blessings came to me. Every day, my life was becoming more joyful, prosperous, and full of love.

As I invited God into my daily life, I felt His presence more and more of the time. When I opened myself to what God had in store for me, I felt peace and love such as I have never known before. As I became more willing to "see" God's wonders - expressed in beautiful ways.

So, get good and humble. Ask God to "help me to be what You want me to be." Admit that you can do better as a human being. I'm not being mean, but you know you can. This meditation technique will slowly but surely give you clear direction - straight into your heart. In the course of reading this book, you have already changed for the better. You have already succeeded in becoming a more relaxed, connected spiritual person. You may not realize it yet, but you have developed all the tools you need to enjoy a daily meditation practice.

"It takes courage to grow up and become who you really are."

~ E.E. Cummings

Give thanks for the amazing feat of strength it took to open up to God or a Higher Power. You have humbly invited Him/Her/It into your life. You are willing to learn about yourself and Eternal Love and Truth. God always listens to the humble heart. The thankful heart. The open heart. YOU have become that open heart.

> *"God, please show me*
> *what you want me to see*
> *and help me to be who*
> *you want me to be."*

EXERCISE:

Your only exercise today is to try all of the steps together. Sit in silence for as long as you are able. Whatever happens, even if supposedly nothing happens, it is perfectly okay. Just relax and bask in the peace and quiet for a few minutes. In our modern world, that is quite an accomplishment in and of itself. Be proud of yourself that you have just taken an important step toward greater relaxation and reconnection to your Creator. Enjoy.

Here are the steps again:

1) Get comfy
2) Take three Cleansing Breaths
3) Develop Gratitude
4) The Divine Invitation -
5) Stay in the Observation Zone (keep looking into the third eye)
6) Show Gratitude Again
7) Document - write down anything you noticed in the Observation Zone, or in

your daily life before and after
meditation.

CHAPTER NINE
WHAT NEXT?

*"When you arise in the morning think
of what a privilege it is to be alive,
to think, to enjoy, to love"
~ Marcus Aurelius*

THINGS THAT MIGHT HAPPEN

Let's talk about some things that you might experience when you begin to meditate. We have already talked about the many wonderful "side-effects" from meditation. Namely, from the first time you sit down and close your eyes, you will begin to reduce stress. You "unplug" a little from the outside world. You let go of the urge to rush around. Ideally, from your first few sessions, you will feel calmer. Some people see beautiful visions or feel a lot of joy quickly in their practice. However, this is rare and should not be expected. In fact, prepare yourself for just the opposite to happen.

Almost everyone goes through an "awkward phase" when they begin anything. Frankly, it might not feel so great at first. Unlike other books on meditation, which paint pictures of only peace, love, and unicorns, this book will be real with you. Let's discuss some things openly, so they don't surprise you, if they happen. The worst thing is to be promised that meditation will help you relax, but when you try it, it causes only frustration. Like most people, your mind may be less like a tranquil bay and more like a stormy sea. I can't promise you smooth sailing right from the start.

But I can promise you that every time you sit down to meditate it will get smoother. For most people, it will take a few weeks to develop the new pattern, this new habit of meditation. No matter how awkward meditation may feel at first, you will get through this beginning phase and enjoy the benefits of meditation before you know it. So, let's be real and get down to it.

When you first begin to meditate, you will feel bored. I mean, extreme boredom. To counteract this, your mind may wander off and find itself in strange places. Weird thoughts will pop up without warning. Your mind will replay scenes from the past, or project out possible scenarios into the future. You might feel like Alice in Wonderland, falling down the rabbit hole. Most people do not enjoy this feeling. Yet, if you take an attitude of curiosity rather than fear, everything will be fine.

If anything comes up from the past, simply acknowledge it and ask God: why am I having this thought now? What can I learn from this situation? Maybe the vision of an old friend means you should give them a call later. Or perhaps a childhood memory will help you with something you're dealing with today. If you freak out, or shut down, you won't get the lesson. Keeping a curious, open mind will help you to view these odd scenarios if they pop up in meditation. The main thing is to remember that you are humbly asking God or Universal Energy, what you are supposed to see. Eventually, random and unnecessary thoughts will fall away, and more meaningful visions will emerge.

When you first start to meditate you will suddenly develop a "To-Do List" that seems so urgent that you must stop what you're doing and run to get it done. This can be something that you always do, and never forget, but it keeps popping up as you meditate. Classic examples are, "Oh gosh, don't forget to pick up the kids at school!"

Sometimes this comes with guilt, such as, "I am so lazy, I didn't finish that pile of dirty laundry." I'm fairly sure a Higher Power does not want you to use this brief, special time to be mean to yourself. No matter what comes up, ask God why He wants you to "see" whatever it is you're seeing. A million things will present themselves. Because you are asking your mind to calm down, your mind will start running around like a three-year-old. You will want to get up and do *anything else but* sit and meditate.

The best way to deal with this is to be gentle with yourself. You can "thank" the random thought and then let it go. For example, "thank you for reminding me about buying peanut butter. I won't forget." If it keeps popping up ask God, "Hum, can you please tell me why this is coming up again? Is there anything important here?" Then, just see what is revealed to you.

We never know if God has some information that we do not have. Oh, wait, yes, we do. God *always* has more information than we do. Please remember that although these things aren't fun, they are just temporary. Beginning a meditation practice is like Spring cleaning your house. It may seem overwhelming at first. There is a lot of old junk up there. Yet, if you do this every day, it will get better. And in the end, you will be so glad you got it done. Meditation is like clearing out your mind.

However, don't get me wrong. You never need to achieve a state of having no thoughts. I suppose some great gurus or monks can attain this, but very few. In this meditation technique you want to learn the grace of thinking… letting go… thinking… letting go…

What should we do when our body seems to rebel against just sitting there? Good question. When most people start to meditate, they often have physical symptoms such as a sudden itch or having to go to the bathroom. This is one reason why the first step "Get Comfy" is so important.

Have a little bit of coffee or tea, and something to keep your tummy from grumbling. Like your mother always said, "Go to the bathroom. Even if you don't think you have to go, just try!" A little preparation before will ensure success.

Now, to the fun stuff. The really magical stuff! After a while, many people will start to see shapes and colors when they look into their third eye. This can be beautiful and sweet. It's God's way of rewarding you for meditating. My advice is to enjoy it. Sit back and luxuriate in it. You do not need to analyze it.

Imagine you are watching the Northern Lights. You wouldn't say, "Well, that green color is too weird, I'm not watching anymore." That would defeat the purpose of reveling in the glory and miracle that you are witnessing. So, in all humility, sit back and enjoy whatever you may see.

My only other advice is to always concentrate on the brightest thing in the center. Even if bright shiny things are happening in the periphery, ignore them. Keep your focus on the center of the third eye. From there, just let it happen. Don't judge it. If something makes you concerned, keep asking why God wants you to see it. You will be shown the reason, eventually. That sense of patience will be developed in time.

In addition, some people may hear music or a tone. It may sound like a flute or oboe, playing off in the distance. Again, it is all perfectly okay. If you wonder about it just keep asking why God wants you to hear it. As Shakespeare said in his play Hamlet, "There is nothing either good or bad, but thinking makes it so." (2)

VARIOUS FEELINGS MAY COME UP

Sometimes people feel a rush of feelings, that perhaps have been pushed down for years. This is usually a good thing. If you feel like crying, go ahead and cry. If you feel like pounding a pillow, go ahead. Sometimes you might even feel the surge of sexual feeling or your heart warming up. All of these things are perfectly normal. New energy is coming into you when you meditate. Trust that your Higher Power or Universal Energy knows what to do, and what areas to send a little "juice."

The most amazing thing to me is when we realize we could improve, we could be better people, better to our community, or whatever the case may be. In meditation sometimes we remember these things or think of them in a new way.

Be humble enough to mean the words, "God help me to be who you want me to be." Yet don't be too hard on yourself, either. You are human. You make mistakes. Every day is a new chance to make it right. Just figure out how to make amends and move on.

Our deepest feelings will become awakened as we meditate. One of the many things that will come up is the subject of forgiveness. Be humble enough to ask God for the reason for the anger or the hurt. Ask God to show you the next appropriate step. As we talked about before, seek out professional support if things become overwhelming. Although you are meditating in silence, there is no reason to suffer in silence.

We all have old resentments and beliefs that in the past people did us wrong. Or we may have some guilt because we hurt someone else. These are "sticky yucky feelings" that we will hold on to with all our might, as if that will help, somehow. It doesn't. We think that if we forgive someone we are letting them "off the hook" and excusing their bad behavior. This isn't true. So we carry around our anger and frustration and fear like a bag of old garbage, slung over our backs.

Forgiveness is not about them, it's about YOU. Do you really want to keep walking around with that bag of garbage on your back all the time? If you are reading this then it's time to let go. It is often the hardest to forgive ourselves.

Sometimes we need to forgive other people, or God Himself, and this takes a concerted effort. Above all, be gentle with yourself. I recommend reading good books and taking workshops on forgiveness.

Rev. Diane Berke, a founder of One Spirit Interfaith Seminary, where I obtained my ordination, has given some of the best information on forgiveness that I have ever experienced. Please do yourself a huge favor and check out one of her YouTube videos, such as "Walking The Path Of Forgiveness" on Dec. 11, 2019. (3) Forgiveness is not a "one and done" type of thing. It is an ongoing process. It is indeed like peeling back the layers of an onion. For those of you who are interested in diving into this important topic, I recommend anything containing information from A Course In Miracles (ACIM) would be a perfect place to start. ACIM is not only a good book, but it offers a new way of thinking and being. It's a philosophy that is beautiful and enriching to any spiritual person, regardless of faith or not. ACIM says, "On forgiveness: Fear condemns and love forgives. Forgiveness thus undoes what fear has produced, returning the mind to the awareness of God." (4)

What if we all decided to forgive, to choose love over fear? Meditation can bring us to this joyful place in our hearts. What if a shift occurred in our entire society which caused the majority of people to meditate? Just as it is now considered to be odd if someone doesn't brush their teeth, what if it was considered odd if someone didn't meditate? Imagine how the world would change! If the majority of people sat in humility for just a few minutes each day and considered how they could become more kind and more aware, there would certainly be less road rage and other negative, impulsive actions. What if most of our leaders practiced some form of meditation? They would begin to work together "across the aisle" more often and offer non-partisan solutions that come from a place of peace and unconditional love. What if everyone took total responsibility for improving themselves, all the time?

Imagine the peaceful world that we could create together!

This brings me to an important point. Now that you are about to "graduate" from being a reader of meditation – to being a True Seeker, you have joined an elite club or society. You are now part of an important community. My advice to all of you, including reminders to myself, is to keep connected to a meditation community. Keep in touch with other spiritual seekers, in whatever way makes sense to you.

Those of us who meditate are at the front lines of the spiritual revolution. Our "weapons" are compassion and unconditional love. With these things in hand and a great deal of patience in our hearts, we will change the world!

Please remember that you are not doing this alone and you are not doing this just for yourself. If enough of us reduce our personal stress, we are, in effect, reducing the stress of the whole world. This is not some fantasy.

Sylvia Boorstein said in her book, "Don't just do something, sit there!" (5) This quote means to take a moment to understand what the next step should be, before taking it. Just like they say on the airplane to put your oxygen mask on first, meditate to care for yourself, first. Once you have helped yourself in this way, you will start to see all kinds of new ways to help others.

At the very least, help other people to meditate. Give them this book or just show them. I have made a commitment to sharing this meditation practice with everyone – as part of my Divine Purpose. If anyone truly can't afford this book, tell them to go to my website (www.revterri.org) and send me a message that they need help purchasing one. Full disclosure, if I get a hundred requests, I probably can't afford that. But you know, one or two here and there is completely within my budget.

Also, I also want everyone to know that the profits from this book will go toward spreading the message of meditation and unconditional love and peace. I am not saying this to toot my own horn, but simply as an example of how God has asked me to share my True Self with others. God will show you what is your special way of growing as a person. You might not write a book, but I am absolutely sure you will do something equally amazing.

I can't put into words the miracles that you are about to enjoy. To keep the momentum going, join, create, or participate in the meditation community of your choice. I have set up my website so that people can discuss spiritual topics and ask questions about meditation. (see info, below) I also have set up a Twitter, Instagram, and Facebook account for people to connect with each other on a variety of platforms. My main point is to include everyone, but especially to include yourself, into a spiritual community of your choice. This is not always easy, but it is always worth it.

You will encounter miracles along the way. If everyone lives a life full of miracles, we will all live in a miraculous place!

Of course, you have a choice of whether to meditate or not. Either way, your relatively frail human existence will contain some tragedy and some great fun. For your sake, I hope more of the latter. I mean to say that no matter what, you will experience every emotion during your time on Earth. A huge, significant human emotion is fear. We are afraid of so many things, including a lack of success and obtaining success. Of being alone or poor or sick. Almost everyone is afraid to die. With daily meditation practice, you will begin to see that there is no reason for fear.

As Franklin D. Roosevelt said in his Inaugural address, "the only thing we have to fear is fear itself." (6) You are about to put down the book and begin a magical journey. Yes, you will still have highs and lows and laughter and tragedy. These are the oceans of life, upon which we all sail.

Meditation will help you become an expert sailor of even the roughest seas. It will offer your life a rudder, so you can live with more direction and purpose. Meanwhile, you will find more peace and joy along the way. There is no end to the wonder, the beauty of life. Through daily meditation, you will become more relaxed and awake. Where there once appeared to be only brick walls in your life, soon you will experience a peaceful yet powerful doorway.

You will "be who God wants you to be." As you become as your Creator made you, you will find the true fountain of love. If you can reduce stress and feel more connected to your True Self, you will naturally share this peace with others. It will flow naturally. The world will be a better place. And isn't that worth five minutes a day?

*For true love is
inexhaustible, the
more you give the
more you have. And if
you go to draw at the
true fountainhead,
the more water you
draw, the more
abundant it's flow."*

*~ Antoine De Saint-
Exupery*

LAST EXERCISE:

Let's bring all the steps together and practice them.

Step One: Get Comfy

Step Two: Cleansing Breaths

Step Three: Develop Gratitude

Step Four: Divine Invitation

Step Five: Observation Zone (of the third eye)

Step Six: Show Gratitude Again

Step Seven: Document Everything.

In this last step, you have become a co-author of this book. The rest is up to you. Here are some suggestions.

1. Write down everything that you will see, feel, and hear during meditation.

2. Add more time, as you are able.

3. Join, or start a meditation community.

4. Get support from a teacher in-person.

5. Keep in touch and get new ideas and connect with others.

6. Please visit the website www.revterri.org for blog posts, informal chats on meditation, interfaith spirituality, ways you can connect with me, ask me questions, share your experiences with me, and other spiritual folks, and gather more information.

7. Last, but never least, be gentle with yourself. You are an evolving manifestation of your Creator. There has never been and there never will be someone exactly like you

"I am not what happened to me, I am what I choose to become."

~ Carl Jung

ADDITIONAL REFERENCES

CHAPTER ONE:

1) Drs. Schucman, H. and Thetford, B. (1975) *A Course In Miracles (ACIM) Combined Volume, Clarification of Terms, Epilogue,* (C-ep.3) Published by the Foundation for Inner Peace

2) Anonymous, (2001) *Alcoholics Anonymous (AA) The Big Book,* Published by Alcoholics Anonymous World Services, Inc. Fourth Edition, p. 59 and from the Alcoholic Anonymous website (https//www.aa.org/pages/en)

3) Katz, S. (2017) *"The Bill Murray Experience"* (Fan Documentary about Bill Murray) Shadow Kamer Films, Written and Directed by Sadie Katz

4) Ram Dass, (1978) *Be Here Now, Illustrated,* Harmony Publishing

5) Brahm, A. quote retrieved Sept. 2020 from Goodreads.com website:

https://www.goodreads.com/quotes
"Meditation is like a gym"
6) Cherokee Legend, *"Story of Two Wolves"* parable, from the website: https//www.firstpeople.us/FP-html-legends/TwoWolves-Cherokee.html
7) Swami Muktananda – quote retrieved Sept. 2020, from Goodreads.com website:
https://www.goodreads.com/quotes
"Your goal is not to battle with the mind"

CHAPTER TWO:
1) King, S., (1999) *Storm of the Century – An Original Screenplay*, Pocket Books
2) New Testament, Revised Standard Version, 2 Timothy 3:16 "The word was with God"
3) Shakespeare, *Hamlet,* quote retrieved Sept. 2020, from Goodreads.com website:
https://www.goodreads.com/quotes,

"there are more things in heaven and earth"

4) Rev. Berke, D. (2018) *Developing & Deepening Your Spiritual Practice, An Interspiritual Approach,* Independently Published

CHAPTER THREE:

1) Drs. Schucman, H. and Thetford, B. (1975) *A Course In Miracles (ACIM) Combined Volume*, published by the Foundation for Inner Peace

2) Sant Darshan Singh, (1978) *The Secret of Secrets, Spiritual Talks*, Sawan Kirpal Publications

3) Mandino, O., quote retrieved Sept. 2020, from Goodreads.com website: https://www.goodreads.com "I will love the light for it shows me the way"

CHAPTER FOUR:

1) Chodron, P. quote retrieved on Sept. 2020 from Goodreads.com website: https://www.goodreads.com

"Meditation is a process of lightening up"

2) Paramahansa Yogananda, (2011) *Autobiography of a Yogi,* Published by Yogoda Satsanga Society of India

3) Okawa, R. (2016) *The Essence of Buddha: The Path to Enlightenment* Irh Press

4) Mokshini, (2017) *blog article re: four main types of meditation,* from website, https:///thebuddistcentre.com/exeter/four-kinds

5) Rabbi Kaplan, A. (1995) *Jewish Meditation: A practical guide,* Schocken Press (1995)

6) Luke, 17:20-21, New Testament, Revised Standard Version, *"Kingdom of God is within you."*

7) Maharishi Mahesh Yogi, (1968) *Transcendental Meditation* ® *Serenity without drugs,* Published by Signet

8) Jon Kabbat-Zinn, Mindfulness Meditation (MBSR) Dept. of

Medicine and the University of Massachusetts (UMASS) Medical Center 1979 and 1982, Department of Medicine and the University of Massachusetts

9) Walsh, R., Shapiro SL. Article: "The meeting of meditative disciplines and Western psychology: a mutually enriching dialogue" *Am. Psychol.* (2006)

10) Jeyning, R., Wallace, R.K., & Beidebach, M. (1992) The physiology of meditation: a review. A wakeful hypometabolic integrated response. *Neuroscience & Biobehavioral Reviews,* 16(3) 415-424

11) Mindfulness.org, Web Article regarding *"Open Monitoring (OM) vs. Focused Attention (FA)"* Website: https://mindfulness.org

12) Kabbat-Zinn, J. quote retrieved Sept. 2020, from Sarahkpeck.com website: https://www.sarahkpeck.com/2015/08/1

5-quotes-on-meditation-and-mindfulness-from-jon-kabat-zin

13) Kabbat-Zinn, J. quote retrieved Sept. 2020, from Goodreads.com website: https://goodreads.com/author/quotes/8750.Jon_Kabat_Zinn

CHAPTER FIVE:

1) Anonymous, AA Big Book, (see above)

2) Mahatma Gandhi, (1999) *"Speech at Prayer Meeting, Sabarmati Ashram Jan. 17, 1930"* text from Vol. 48, p. 242 in Gandhi, Mohandas Karamchand. The collected works of Mahatma Gandhi (electronic book). New Delhi: Publications Division Government of India. Archived from the original on 2008-05-09.)

3) Author Unknown, Translation by Griffith, R. (2017) *Gayatri Mantra, The Rig Veda: Complete (Illustrated)* Published by CreateSpace Independent Publishing Platform

4) Buddhist prayer retrieved Sept. 2020, from Xavier and jesuitresource.org website: https://www.xavier.edu/jesuitresource/online-resources/prayer-index/buddhist-prayers "May all beings have happiness"

5) Rabbi Hakotun, M. prayer retrieved Sept. 2020 from wexnermedical.osu.edu website: https://wexnermedical.osu.edu/-/media/files/wexnermedical/faith-specific-prayers "When I walk through the woods"

6) Lakota prayer, retrieved Sept. 2020 from Sapphyr.net website: http://www.sapphyr.net/natam/quotes-nativeamerican.htm

7) Rumi, retrieved Sept. 2020 from Shortpoems.org website: https//www.shortpoems.org/poets/rumi/short_poems_rumi

8) The Prophet Muhammad (Peace Be Upon His Name) from the Qur'an:

(2005) *A new translation* by M.A.S. Abdel Haleem, Oxford University Press

9) The Qur'an: see above

10) Luke and Matthew, *The Lord's Prayer,* The New Testament, Revised Standard Version,

11) Chinese proverb: "Don't push the river, it flows by itself."

12) Serenity Prayer – found in Narcotics Anonymous literature. (1976) from *NA White Booklet.* Narcotics Anonymous World Services, Inc.

13) Kierkegaard, S. quote retrieved Sept. 2020, from Goodreads.com website: https://www.goodreads.com/quotes "on prayer"

CHAPTER SIX:

1) Dr. Chopra, D. quote retrieved Sept. 2020, from Goodreads.com website: https://www.goodreads.com/quotes "Meditation is a vital way to purify and quiet the mind"

2) Schatz, C. (2011) Mindfulness meditation improves connections in the brain, Atricle, Harvard Health Publishing, Harvard Medical school, https://www.health.harvard.edu/blog/mindfulness-meditation-improves-connections-in-the-brain also (April 2011) Mindfulness meditation practice changes the brain article from Harvard Women's Health Watch, https://www.health.harvard.edu./mind-and-mood/mindfulness-meditation-practice-changes-the-brain

3) Mayo Clinic Staff, *Meditation: A simple, fast way to reduce stress*" from the website https//www.mayoclinic.org/tests-procedures/meditation/in-depth/meditation

4) Osho, quote retrieved Sept. 2020, from Goodreads.com website: http://www.goodreads.com/quotes "Touch your inner space"

CHAPTER SEVEN:

1) Blake, W., (1982) *Complete Poetry and Prose of William Blake,* Compiled by Erdman, D. and Bloom H., Published by Anchor

2) Rumi, quote retrieved Sept. 2020, from Goodreads.com website: https://www.goodreads.com/author/quotes/875661.Rumi "Come out of the circle of time"

CHAPTER EIGHT:

1) Einstein, A. (2000) *The Expanded Quotable Einstein,* Princeton University Press, p.202 "I want to know how God created this world"

2) Cummings, E.E., quote retrieved Sept.2020, from Goodreads.com website: https://www.goodreads.com/quotes "Grow up and become who you are"

CHAPTER NINE:

1) Marcus Aurelius, quote retrieved Sept. 2020 from Goodreads.com website: https://www/goodreads.com/quotes "Privilege to be alive"

2) Shakespeare, Hamlet, "There's nothing either good or bad" quote retrieved Sept. 2020, from Goodreads.com website: https://www.goodreads.com/quotes

3) Rev. Berke, D., (Dec. 11, 2019) *Walking the Path of Forgiveness,* You Tube video

4) See Above, A Course In Miracles (ACIM) "On forgiveness" W – pl.46.2.2-3, published by the Foundation for Inner Peace,

5) Boorstein, S., (1996) *Don't Just Do Something, Sit There: A mindfulness retreat*, First Edition, Published by HarperOne

6) Roosevelt, F.D., (1938) *Inaugural Address, March 4, 1933,* as published in Samuel Rosenman, ed. *The Public Papers of Franklin D. Roosevelt, Volume Two: The Year of Crisis, 1933* New York: Random House

7) Antoine De Saint-Exupery Quotes (n.d) BrainyQuote.com, Retrieved

Sept. 2020, from BrainyQuote.com website: https://www.brainyquote.com/quotes/antoine_de_saintexupery_401692 "For true love is inexhaustible…fountainhead of love"

8) Carl Jung, from Goalcast.com, retrieved Sept.2020, from Goalcast.com website: https://www.goalcast.com/2018/01/23/15_enlightening-carl-jung-quotes "I am not what happened to me… "

Here is my example of "Developing Gratitude"

I am so blessed for everyone who has supported me as I gave birth to this book. So many have kept me company along the way or had some special part to play. I am so thankful for my work helping those experiencing poverty and homelessness. Most of all, I am thankful for all the amazing people in my life. I will just list a few who helped me find my True Self - although in my heart, there are dozens.

First, I give thanks for my parents, Marilyn and David Meigs. They taught me that helping others is more important than all the riches in the world. I am grateful for my close-knit loving family: Tom, Jim, Jane, Steven and Eric Meigs. I am also so lucky to have many wonderful aunts, uncles and cousins. I especially appreciate some cousins who are more like sisters: Susan, Debbi and Kathleen. I also honor those who have passed, such as my beloved grandparents. My dear family - your place in my heart is forever.

I am eternally gratefully for my dearest friend since high school, a prolific writer and now my publisher, L.M.Pampuro. Your patience and dedication has meant the world to me. This book would not exist without you. Thank you so much for everything!

Speaking of the best of friends, I wish to thank Tim for encouraging and supporting me in a million ways. I am also so happy that Brian, a dear friend for years, has also become my most dedicated literary friend. And I am grateful for Faith and Steve; your warmth and hospitality always make me happy.

A group of beautiful, smart, sassy women make up what we affectionately call the "LoL club." Beth, Kristen and Debbie Lynn – thank you for your wisdom, humor and strength. I also want to thank so many other dear people in my life who have danced with me on this journey. You know who you are and how much I love you.

I give thanks for all my wise and wonderful spiritual teachers. Heartfelt thanks to Rev. Wayne Gill, Sant Darshan Singh, Ram Dass, Rabbi Myron Kinberg and Marianne Williamson, among many others. I will always have a special place in my heart for everyone at One Spirit Interfaith Seminary, especially Donna and Dale and my teachers, Rev. Diane Berke and Rev. David Wallace.

Lastly, but not least, I thank you, the reader. You have joined me on a path of self-exploration. The words "thank you" do not accurately describe how much I feel for all of you. With you, life makes sense. Keep exploring your True Self and so will I. And I will meet you there, in the center of peace and joy.

For more information please visit:
RevTerri.org

RevTerri2020@gmail.com